A Cancer Warrior's Perspective

A Practical Guide for Loved Ones to Support Young Adults Fighting Cancer

Janice Armbrust

ISBN: 979-8-218-56634-0

Contents

Introduction

If you're reading this book, it probably means that someone close to you has been diagnosed with cancer. If that's the case: I'm sorry—that sucks. You might be wondering what someone experiencing a cancer diagnosis is going through and what on earth you can do to help them. The purpose of this book is to offer you some ideas based on my own personal experience as a young adult with brain cancer. Hopefully my book can help you support your loved one, friend, or even colleague.

In the following chapters, I will go through a few milestones in my cancer journey to give you an idea of what such a journey can look like. Each chapter ends with a few practical ideas of how cancer patients can be supported. As you read, please keep two things in mind: First, I am not a doctor. This book is not intended to give any medical advice at all. Since this book is primarily for friends, relatives, colleagues, and other support networks of cancer patients, I will keep the medical aspects of my journey as brief as possible and will not go into extensive details of my own diagnosis or treatment. Second, every person is different. I can only offer insights based on my own personal journey and preferences. While I hope that you'll find my recommendations helpful, they may not all apply to your loved one, friend, or colleague. Every cancer, every situation, and every story is unique. *So then, why am I even writing this book?*

Since, according to the World Health Organization, the number of cancer cases has been growing globally for the past years, more and more people will need support from their friends, families, colleagues, communities, and caregivers. Support systems and social connections make a huge difference in a cancer journey. The support we receive from our social relationships is a significant protector for our health. With this book I want to enable more people to give support in meaningful ways.

In addition, according to recent research from the American Cancer Society, rates for certain types of cancer are rising, specifically among *young* patients. While I was going through the early stages of my journey, I found that there were not enough resources that address the specific issue of being a young adult with cancer. Imagine finding out about a severe health crisis in your late twenties, when you're potentially just about to solidify your career path, establish financial stability, plan your family, or get a true understanding of what your priorities are in life. Having cancer at this stage in your life comes with its own unique set of challenges. Therefore, I decided to share the challenges I was experiencing and how my friends, family, and colleagues supported me through them.

Last but not least, just as I am not a doctor, I am also not a therapist (though I did study psychology in college). If you are a cancer patient or a caregiver, or simply struggling with something emotionally, please put this book to the side and seek professional help.

Good luck and positive thoughts.

Terminology

Before we dive in, I need to introduce the term "cancer warrior." Since the cancer patient in question could be your friend, wife, husband, partner, another family member, colleague, or even neighbor, I wanted to find a word that encompasses all these relationships. The most obvious solution could have been to just stick to "cancer patient"; it's simple, but sometimes it felt too clinical and didn't quite do the trick. After considering other names like "cancer survivor" (too premature), "cancer thriver" (too positive), "cancer sufferer" (too negative), and "cancer fighter" (too aggressive), I landed on "cancer warrior." This term has been criticized in recent years, mostly because the word "warrior" makes it seem like cancer patients *choose* to join a fight—and if we fight hard enough, we may win. This can put additional pressure on the patient or create a false sense of hope for their loved ones when the outcome of this disease is often out of our direct control.

Despite these nuances, I am using the term "cancer warrior" throughout this book to refer to the person you care about who has cancer. Personally, my cancer journey has made me feel like a warrior in many instances, and like many others I find the term energizing. Be aware that others may prefer different terms.

Chapter 1: Just Another Tuesday

"I'll be right back" is what I told my team at work before I left for a doctor's appointment that would change my life forever. It was Tuesday, August 10, 2021. The day had started just like any other Tuesday. I kicked off my morning with a run around the Central Park Reservoir and a healthy breakfast in my tiny studio apartment on New York City's Upper East Side. I had moved to New York from Germany in 2019. Living in the US was a lifelong dream of mine, and two and a half years in I still couldn't believe that I got to call this place home.

Next on my morning routine: several virtual meetings with my team in India and my clients in California. Due to the COVID-19 pandemic, I was working from home after years of traveling around the world for various consulting projects. Before the pandemic I used to get on a plane every Monday morning to collaborate in person with my clients and teams before flying back to New York on Thursday nights. But now, just like so many other people, I had turned my small bedroom into an office and had become the proud owner of a proper desk. It was at this desk that I told my team, "I'll be right back. I'm just getting an MRI done." We said goodbye, and I shut down my work laptop. Little did I know that I wouldn't turn it back on for another six months.

MRI stands for Magnetic Resonance Imaging. The output looks like a black-and-white picture of the tissue inside your body. People get MRIs done for all sorts of health conditions and injuries. At this point I had never gotten an MRI before, so I wasn't sure what to expect. All I knew was that MRI machines were supposedly loud and made some people feel claustrophobic.

I was sitting in the waiting room, constantly checking the time to make sure I could make it back home for my next meeting, when a nurse called my name. I changed into a hideous hospital gown, put my belongings in a locker, and was led into a room where I was instructed to lie down on a tablelike structure. A nurse desperately fumbled to get an intravenous (IV) line into my annoyingly small veins, which they would use to give me a contrast dye if needed. MRIs can be done in two ways: with or without contrast. From a patient's perspective, getting the contrast dye simply adds a few extra steps to your MRI process, like getting the IV line inserted in your arm. Contrast helps the radiologist interpret the MRIs to find small differences between healthy and unhealthy tissues in your body.

While the nurse inspected her IV, a technician made sure my MRI experience was as comfortable as possible. He propped my knees up with a pillow and provided me ear plugs and headphones to block out some of the banging and chirping sounds from the MRI machine. He also handed me a small ball and instructed me to press it if I needed any help while the MRI was running. Finally, the technician asked what music I would prefer to listen to during my MRI—a question that took me by surprise. Leading up to an MRI, patients must answer many questions to ensure that the imaging can be done safely. Such questions are usually about your health condition, metals in your body, or a potential pregnancy. I did not expect my taste in music to be a topic of discussion today. To avoid delaying the process, I told the technician simply to play something calming. A big mistake, I realized moments later as jazzy piano music started to invade my ears . . . The technician and I apparently had very different definitions of "calming." I lay on the patient table as it moved into the MRI machine, and a few minutes later I heard the technician's voice over my headphones, informing me that he would now start the MRI and I should try to keep my head perfectly still. I closed my eyes as the muffled sounds of the MRI device began beeping to life around me.

Over the next twenty-five minutes, while trying to expand my musical horizons to the wonders of jazz, I reflected on the events that led me into this weird machine in the first place.

It had all started a few weeks earlier. Out of nowhere, I had trouble hearing with my right ear. After a few days of self-medication, equalization attempts, and tea, I saw an ear doctor who confirmed that my ears were perfectly fine and suspected that my symptoms were stress related. This was not implausible since I was hustling at work and in life—in between sixty-hour work weeks, I was enjoying the summertime with short weekend trips, hiking and rock climbing all over the US. But my symptoms got worse; on a thirty-five-mile backpacking trip in Washington State, I started having spells of dizziness and nausea. The sensation was so unusual that I made an appointment with my primary care doctor in New York while I was still at the Seattle airport. My doctor initially ordered me to get a COVID test; after all, we were still in a global pandemic. But the test came back negative, and a few headache- and anxiety-filled weeks later, I found myself here, in an MRI machine, listening to jazz . . .

My headphones crackled and I heard the technician say, "Ms. Armbrust? We'll give you the contrast now. You'll feel a cold trickle in your right arm. Another eight minutes, and you should be all done. Are you doing OK?" "Mm-hmm," I responded, trying to keep my head still.

In general, I was doing more than OK—I was doing great. Outside of my weird symptoms, I was probably the happiest person on the planet. I had made my lifelong dream come true at the age of twenty-eight, when I moved to New York. I had amazing friends in several countries across the globe. Yes, I worked a lot, but as a workaholic that only energized me, and the salary allowed me to travel and live a privileged life. To top all of this off, I got to share my life with my wonderful significant other, Jeff, who I had been dating for one and a half years at the time. I truly couldn't think of anything amiss. I wasn't only OK— I was ridiculously happy and eager to see what else life had in store for me.

Eventually the patient table emerged from the MRI machine and a nurse helped me up from my lying position. She announced that the MRI was done and I could change back into my regular clothes. A few moments later, I was ready to head back to work and go on with my regular life.

But just as I was about to leave the building, the radiologist caught up with me. "Ms. Armbrust? You should call your doctor as soon as possible!" My heart sank. I had a small suspicion that was not quite normal. I wanted to find out more from him, but he had already turned around to review another scan of another brain.

I tried to remain calm and decided to grab lunch somewhere first. Then I would call the doctor and get back to my meetings.

However, while I was still debating what kind of protein I wanted in my salad, my doctor called and offered to make an appointment for as soon as I could come in. I got increasingly worried. This did not seem normal at all. I called Jeff, who immediately left work so he could join me for the appointment. I tried to convince him that this surely wouldn't be worth missing a day of work, but he was determined. He was working at a hospital within walking distance of my doctor's office, so I agreed to meet him there shortly. Salad in hand, I started speedwalking to my doctor's office while texting a few friends who knew of my recent health issues:

> "I'm losing it. They found something in the MRI, but they can't tell me what it is yet. It sounds like there is some sort of swelling in my brain. I'm freaking out. I'm running to see my doctor now."

Thirty minutes later, Jeff and I were sitting in my doctor's office. Jeff was holding my hand and rubbing my back, trying to calm me down while I went through an entire box of tissues in scared anticipation of the doctor's arrival. Once she entered the room, she cut straight to the chase. "I'm not a neurologist, and you'll want to meet with one as soon as possible. But what I can tell you is that there seems to be a mass in your brain. I already called a neurosurgeon who can see you tomorrow. She'll be better equipped to decide what to do next."

I tried to focus on her words, but that was a tough undertaking as I was in absolute shock. I kept asking, "What kind of mass? Is it cancer? What's going to happen to me?" Questions that a primary care doctor wouldn't know how to answer. In fact, at the time no one would be able to answer these questions without taking a proper look inside my brain. There are now new innovations emerging that may one day be able to help diagnose brain tumors without a biopsy, but when I started my brain cancer journey, a biopsy was the only way to get clear answers. Many tears, unanswered questions, and confused, helpless gazes exchanged between Jeff and me later, we left the doctor's office.

Over the course of one afternoon, my life had been flipped upside down. I was scared and in shock. All I knew for sure was that I would see a neurosurgeon the next day. I called my supervisor at work, warning him that I might be out for a few days. In the meantime, Jeff picked up prescribed steroids for me at the pharmacy that would help reduce the swelling in my brain. Unsurprisingly, there is not a lot of room in the human skull for anything to start swelling or growing there. Taking steroids was the one and only action within my power while we waited for the doctors to figure out the next steps.

Jeff and I also had one additional last mission for the day: We needed to head back to the imaging center where I had gotten my MRI so we could get a CD of my brain scan. Yes, a compact disc—apparently those still exist. In fact, I have collected around fifty CDs with images of my brain over the past three years! CDs seem to be the most effective way for doctors to receive high-quality images in a secure manner. So, Jeff and I stormed into the imaging facility a few minutes before closing time. We somehow managed to convince the frowning receptionist to call up a medical records person and produce a copy of my scans. I could probably write a whole separate book on the importance of securing medical records and the challenges in navigating access to them, but the most important thing to know is patients have a right to their medical records. Medical providers are required to share them with you when you request them. While some can easily be accessed online others, such as MRI images, often take time and sometimes even money to receive them. Twenty minutes and ten dollars later, the receptionist handed us an envelope before announcing that her office was now closed. The envelope contained the CD as well as a printed copy of the MRI report, which is a summary of the radiologist's findings based on his analysis of my scan. Jeff and I headed home and read the report over and over, trying to deduct any additional information from it, but the highly medical gibberish didn't make any sense to us and our heads were still swirling from everything that had happened that day.

I honestly cannot remember much of what we did the rest of the evening. All I remember is feeling a mix of panic and hope, fearing the worst but clinging on to everlasting optimism. And I remember Jeff continuing to promise, "We are in this together, and we will get through whatever this is." And with that, the most memorable Tuesday of my life finally came to an end.

How you can support:

Realistically, there's not a lot that most of my friends, relatives, or other supporters could have done on day one of my journey, except be present.

☞ Be present physically: I absolutely needed Jeff in this first appointment to console me, share the confusion with me, and simply hug me. If I didn't have Jeff, I probably would have wanted a friend to spend the evening with me (or even stay overnight). If I had been by myself, I would have absolutely fallen apart with panic. This, of course, depends on how close you are with your warrior. If it's appropriate, offer to be there.

☞ Be present emotionally: The few friends I had texted during the day immediately showered me with compassionate responses, like this one: Sending such a big hug right now. If you need anything I'm here. I can only imagine how scared and stressed you're feeling right now. I know Jeff is with you, but if you need/want someone to join at your appointment tomorrow, I will make the time. This is exactly the type of response that I needed in this moment: something understanding, supportive, and acknowledging that this is a scary situation, but not overdramatizing the unknown.

Chapter 2: What the F**k Just Happened

The next day was pure chaos. Jeff and I were grabbing subway trains, cabs, and even Citi Bikes to sprint across New York City, from my apartment to his apartment, to the hospital, to the pharmacy, to a FedEx store, and back to the hospital. The day was a complete blur, except for the anticipated appointment with my neurosurgeon.

We came prepared with pen and paper and a list of questions: What could this thing in my brain be? ("Very likely a tumor, but it's unclear if it's malicious or benign.") How big is this thing, whatever it is? ("About the size of a golf ball.") Is the dosage of steroids that my primary care physician prescribed reasonable? ("Yes. We need the swelling to go down because pressure in your brain is dangerous and ultimately can be fatal.") Do I need surgery? ("Yes. We scheduled you for Monday.")

Monday . . . That was only five days away!

We then went over all the risks of having a brain surgery, the risks of not having the surgery, and everything I'd need to do to prepare for the surgery. It was hard to focus. All I kept thinking was, 'This woman will cut my brain open in five days!' Out of curiosity I asked her whether she would shave my head. I've always had short hair and was kind of hoping that I'd at least get a new hairstyle out of this whole situation. But unexpectedly, my neurosurgeon's signature move was to operate while leaving the hair intact. An image of brain mass tangled in my short mop of strawberry blonde hair entered my head. I pushed it away and decided just to follow her process. She seemed competent and had a professional, hands-on energy about her. And what other option did I have other than to trust her? After all, this woman would be performing fairly complex surgery on me in a few days.

But there was one option I did have: to get a second opinion. And even though things were moving extremely fast, Jeff and I wanted to get one. We had no doubt that my neurosurgeon was great . . . but it just seemed crazy to undergo such an intense procedure based on one single person's assessment. Luckily, by odd chance, Jeff was friends with a neurosurgeon who lived far away. So, we ran to get more CDs and quickly mailed them to Jeff's friend over night. Ultimately, he confirmed everything our neurosurgeon had said, done, and planned to do. He also let us know that neurologists and neurosurgeons often work in teams and are all part of a tumor board—a group of physicians and scientists that comes together regularly to discuss treatment options for their patients. So, the decision to do surgery this quickly likely had been made by a team of experts. There was no further doubt—I would undergo brain surgery in five days. Jeff and I set off to tackle the lengthy pre-surgery to-do list:

- ✓ Inform work that I'd be out until further notice.

- ✓ Figure out whether I have short-term disability insurance and how it works.

- ✓ Appoint a health proxy, someone who would make decisions on my behalf if I were no longer able to make decisions on my own (for example, if I fell into a coma).

- ✓ Decide and document which medical procedures I consent to, in case I need life-prolonging interventions.

- ✓ Inform my health insurance of the upcoming procedure and ensure I was covered.

- ✓ Make a list of key contacts and determine who would receive news from whom.

- ✓ Find a hospital interpreter who can translate any complications to my German relatives.

- ✓ Get tested once more for COVID-19 and a few other potentially surgery-preventing diseases.

- ✓ Pick up an antibacterial ointment to prevent infections after surgery.

- ✓ Get some special antibacterial shampoo.

- ✓ Pack a hospital bag.

These five days between the neurosurgeon appointment and my brain surgery were some of the busiest and most emotional days of my entire life. I don't know how I would have done it without the help of so many loved ones in my life. My lengthy and frankly scary to-do list had one advantage, though—I had absolutely no time to fully process my one main thought: WHAT THE F**CK JUST HAPPENED?! Every time I paused, I would start crying, and all the worries and concerns would come crashing down on me. But there was no time to stop. Because in between all the errands we were burning through, I also felt that I had to tell my closest friends—and, most importantly, my mom.

How you can support:

Remember that every person is different. While I think it's helpful to *offer* the things I note below, all you can do is offer and respect the response. Keep this in mind as we continue through the rest of the book—and respect your warrior's choices.

☞ Come to appointments: The beginning of any health journey can be extremely overwhelming. The decisions that I had to make while still processing my own emotions under time pressure, all while my own future had just potentially changed forever . . . it's an incredibly complex situation. Having a second set of eyes and ears to ask questions and take notes is extremely helpful.

☞ Help with surgery preparation: You can ask what your warrior is doing to prepare for surgery. Did they receive a formal list from their doctor that you can help tackle? If they didn't receive one, would it be helpful for you to find one online and discuss it? Can you help to get some items checked off the list?

☞ Talk about the surgery—and listen: I like to talk to my friends about my thoughts and feelings. The few ones who already knew about my MRI gently asked me all sorts of questions about the upcoming surgery: "How long will it be?" "Do you like the surgeon? What is she like?" "Do you know what floor you'll be on?" "What are you looking forward to after the surgery? Will you be able to eat pizza? I can make a reservation for us in a few weeks." I liked their neutral, fact-oriented questions. Telling them what I knew helped me to process and prepare. But I also know that some patients prefer not to talk about their surgeries, and that is OK as well.

Chapter 3: "Mom, I Need to Tell You Something…"

How do you tell people who love you that your life has just been flipped entirely upside down? And who do you tell? Do you even have to tell anyone? New York is far away from my hometown—could I keep this from people so I wouldn't worry them? The prospect of having to break the news to my friends, and especially my mother, was just about as scary as the surgery itself. I knew the conversations would be hard and I would cry. And, even worse, I knew that I would likely make my friends and family cry. Most of my close New York friends knew that I had gotten an MRI and had proactively requested updates. They were already along for my emotional ride. But I hadn't even mentioned my MRI to my mom or any of my German friends because I simply had not expected anything to be this dramatically wrong with me. Now that I was scheduled for a rather complicated surgery, I knew I needed to tell them as soon as possible. The thought of waiting and eventually telling people I love something along the lines of, "Oh, hey, by the way, I had brain surgery last week, but it's all good now," seemed impossible. I ended up making some dreaded calls, but not without a plan.

I had to have Jeff by my side for the most difficult calls, and I wanted to make sure my loved ones also had someone supporting them by their side. I texted my mom's boyfriend first:

> "Are you able to talk in the next 1–2 hours? I don't want to worry you, but something health related has happened and I want to tell Mom. But I want to make sure you're next to her when I tell her. In short, I'll have to get surgery on Monday and there could be some complications."

We arranged a time when I would call my mom and he would be sitting next to her to comfort her when needed. There are pros and cons to this process, but I'm glad I did it like this. My mom and I both cried in the arms of our significant others and ended the conversation joking over the prospect that my surgeon could accidentally trap my hair inside my brain.

Since this approach worked well, I followed a similar pattern for my very best friends. Other close friends, who I decided needed to know prior to the surgery, received a text along the lines of this:

> "Hi, I'm sorry, but I'm bearing bad news. So, if this is not a good time, please read this a bit later…
> I wanted you to know this but won't have time to talk much about it before it happens. Here it goes: I found out Wednesday that I likely have a tumor in my brain, and they are taking it out on Monday. I don't know much more than that yet (benign, malicious, next steps, etc.). For now, all I know is that I'm receiving brain surgery on Monday, and then I'll spend a few days at the hospital. Jeff and everybody here are taking amazing care of me. I'm currently doing OK, except that I'm pretty scared of what all of this means. We'll likely know more in 1.5 weeks. I just wanted you to know before it happens. Wish me luck!"

There were many friends I didn't reach out to prior to the surgery. This didn't mean that I didn't love them; I simply ran out of the time, energy, and mental capacity to tell more people. I know patients who, even after half a year into their cancer treatment, had told only their significant others and parents about their health issues. It is a very personal decision. I did what felt right for me and my loved ones—I've always thrived on the support from my friends, family, and coworkers and knew that I was going to need it now more than ever. Their love, encouraging texts, distracting phone calls, walks, hugs, and voice messages were what got me through the weekend before my surgery.

Jeff and I rounded out Sunday evening with tears, smiles, and more tears. Then it was time to go to bed and try to get some sleep.

How you can support:

☞ Offer to spread the word: Only if your warrior agrees, you can help share the news with mutual friends and suggest the messaging that you would use.

☞ Don't take it personally: If you're the one receiving updates from a mutual friend, do not interpret this to mean anything about your relationship with your warrior. Their emotional, physical, or time capacity may have just hindered them from telling you personally. Once you know, unless you're told otherwise, reach out and let your warrior know you're thinking of them.

☞ Respond (compassionately): Learning that a loved one is going through a tough situation sucks. It's often difficult to find the right words. What matters is that you do respond, even if you don't know how you should. It's totally fine to admit that. For example: "I'm not sure what to say right now, but I want you to know that I care and I'm always here whatever you need." You don't have to comment on anything else. No "That sounds horrible," or "My uncle had brain surgery, and it was no big deal." Avoid dramatizations, comparisons, or downplaying.

☞ Give space: Your warrior is going through a lot right now, and you probably have many questions and want to be there for them. You can let them know exactly that and say: "I have a lot of questions but know that you probably need your space right now to get everything sorted. Just let me know if you do want to talk or if there is anything I can do for you right now. Love you!"

☞ Expect "I don't know": It's frustrating for everyone involved to lack information, but especially in this early stage, your warrior likely doesn't have all the answers to your questions. Accept that this is the case and don't dig any further. You may even want to change the subject so that you don't send your warrior spiraling over too many unknowns.

Chapter 4: Get This Thing Out of My Head

Sunday night turned out to be a rather sleepless night, mostly because I was nervous. I had never undergone surgery before and didn't know what to expect. I had already asked my neurosurgeon all the questions that I could possibly think of, and there was nothing else for me to prepare. But still, here I was the night before, worrying about all the unknowns. What would the operating room look like? Would the surgery start at the scheduled time? Where would I wake up after the surgery? How much pain would I be in? What if there were complications and I woke up unable to speak or walk? What if the anesthesia didn't work on me and I woke up during the procedure? Would Jeff and my mom get all the information they needed? What if I had forgotten to complete one of the preparation activities during the last few hectic days?

Over and over again, I went through the preoperative checklist in my head, anxious that I had unknowingly done something wrong that would prevent me from getting my potentially life-saving surgery. But I had taken all the prescribed medications and ointments, avoided prohibited medications like blood thinners, and showered with the special antibacterial soap. All the paperwork was completed, and all the communications were in place. My overnight bag was packed and sitting in front of my apartment door, and I had stopped eating twelve hours prior to the scheduled surgery, as required. The fasting part additionally prevented me from sleeping: I was getting increasingly hungry, but the next meal was many long hours (and a brain surgery) away.

Also, I was nervous that I would accidentally oversleep and miss my surgery entirely—a scenario that was quite unlikely, given the fifteen alarms Jeff and I had collectively set on three separate devices.

I was almost relieved when it was finally time to get up and leave for the hospital. Jeff and I checked in at the admissions office at 6:00 a.m. sharp. While our phones buzzed away with early morning well-wishes and positive vibes from friends and family, we completed all the admissions activities: more paperwork. After a short wait (which felt like hours to me), we were led into a pre-procedure unit. We sat in a small room that quickly became crowded with friendly nurses who prepared me for the surgery. They started by taking my weight, measuring my heart rate and oxygen level, and making sure I didn't have a fever. Next up was another game of "Try to find the vein." Since I hadn't been allowed to eat or hydrate for hours, placing an IV in my arm became quite the mission. Eventually my vein played along, and after a few more forms and one more pregnancy test, it was finally time to head toward the operating room. I had to part ways from Jeff because visitors were not allowed in the operating room. He gave me one last kiss and we assured each other that "everything will be OK and I'll see you in a few hours."

I hopped into a comfy hospital bed and then met the next team in this process: my anesthesiologists. They went over the details of the anesthesia as well as all the potential risks that come with receiving it. At this point I had heard it all before, but no matter how scary the risks sounded, I knew I had no other choice than to go through with the surgery. Something was growing in my brain, and it needed to come out. Today. Now. I was ready. I signed one last document consenting to the anesthesia and was finally wheeled into the operating room.

When I was a kid, I had an operating room toy set from Playmobil. As I entered the operating room, this toy set popped into my head. The trays, the giant lamp, the people in green scrubs and surgical caps . . . it was all here. The room felt busy but organized. Nurses and assistants shuffled around, moving devices and talking in calm but urgent voices, getting everything set up around me.

The neurosurgeon I had met only five days ago was in the room as well. She explained the procedure to me one last time: The surgery was expected to take only three hours. While some types of brain surgery require patients to be awake and responsive (yikes!), I would be asleep for the full duration of mine. The surgeon was going to remove a piece of my skull and as much of the mass in my brain as possible without harming the parts providing critical functions. Once that was done, she would use a titanium plate to close the hole in my skull and staple my skin back together so that everything could heal. She asked whether I had any last questions. I only had one: "Are you sure you don't want to shave my hair?" She laughed and confirmed that she had no intentions of shaving anything. While I was once again wondering how on earth she'd manage to keep my hair out of my skull, someone explained that they would now start with the anesthesia. They instructed me to inhale deeply through a mask over my nose and mouth. I briefly remember thinking, 'This is it. Get this thing out of my head!' Then I fell asleep.

☞ Be the cheer squad: The day of my surgery was the day I needed the encouraging types of messages the most. Before and after this day, I found it hard to tell if I wanted people to cheer me up or commiserate with me. But on the surgery day, I just needed everyone to text me something like: Don't respond to this. I just want to let you know that you're freakin' strong and tough, and YOU CAN DO THIS!

☞ Support the caregiver: While I slept in my cozy hospital bed, unconscious from the anesthesia, Jeff waited outside the room. I cannot even begin to imagine how nerve-racking that must have been for him. Fortunately, he had two friends come by the hospital to distract him and stay with him until he was notified that the surgery had gone well and he could come to my room.

☞ Provide distraction: If appropriate, offer to join your cancer warrior at the hospital before or after the surgery to provide distraction. Make it clear that you won't be offended if your presence is not needed. You don't have to stay long either. Find out what your warrior needs to feel supported in this moment, especially if they don't have a family member or someone else joining them at the hospital.

Chapter 5: Rest, Recover, and Wait

A few hours later, I started to wake up. It took me a moment to get oriented. I found myself in a hospital room with lots of beeping machines and Jeff sitting in a chair nearby. He called for a nurse as I, still very groggy from the anesthesia, slowly took stock of my body. I had IVs in my arms and was attached to a bag containing a clear liquid. An itching on my chest quickly gave away that someone must have equipped me with sticky electrodes to measure my heart rate and rhythm. The heart rate machine next to me confirmed this suspicion. My right finger was attached to one of those tiny devices that measure oxygen levels. So far, it was what I expected.

Next, I realized that someone had wrapped my calves in a sort of massaging device to prevent blood clots. Less expected and less comfortable. However, by far the most uncomfortable of all of my new body attachments was the catheter that must have been inserted into my bladder while I was asleep. I never had one of these catheters before, and the experience was immediately annoying and very unpleasant. But none of this compared to the soreness in my head, neck, jaw, and throat. I had expected to wake up with a bit of a headache, given that someone had just sliced open my skull and removed a chunk of tissue from my brain. But what were all of these other sensations about?

The first nurse who came by offered some answers. "Sometimes they have to cut through jaw muscle when they access your skull. That's probably why your jaw hurts. It could also be from the intubation, which may very likely be the reason why your throat feels so sore. Lots of patients wake up with neck pain because of the way their heads were propped up during the surgery." At this time additional people in white coats, presumably doctors, walked into the room, so I didn't have any time to dwell on this jaw-muscle massacre that the nurse had just insinuated.

What followed was my first ever neuro check. Doctors or their assistants conduct these checks to test your neurological abilities. One of them instructed, "Close your eyes and touch your finger to your nose and then to my finger here. Good . . . Follow my fingers with your eyes . . . Close your eyes and hold your arms up straight as if you were holding a pizza box." When I pointed out that no one in the world would ever hold a pizza box like this, they seemed satisfied with my current mental abilities given the circumstances. Of course, I was still pretty drugged, so my brain was working slowly and I was speaking in a sluggish way. My eyesight was blurry and very sensitive to light. But I was told that this would improve over the course of the next days (which it did, for the most part). Overall, I was doing pretty well for someone who had just come out of brain surgery!

The day continued with me drifting in and out of sleep, trying to ignore the pain and the beeping of all the machines. Occasionally doctors would wake me up to complete more tests and share additional updates with me. I was told that the surgery was a great success and they were able to remove almost the entire tumor!

Jeff was in charge of communicating the good news to my mom and closest friends. I had provided him with their phone numbers and let them know that he would be the one to keep them posted during my surgery. In fact, we ended up continuing this system for a few more weeks after the surgery because looking at screens was incredibly uncomfortable for me, and talking for a long time (especially on the phone) felt exhausting. While Jeff spread the great news to everyone, we tried to learn any additional information from the doctors, most importantly the answers to questions like: What kind of tumor are we talking about? Is it malicious or benign? Will it come back? Will it kill me?

But, as expected, there was nothing more they could tell me at this point, not until the pathology results came back. My tumor was apparently on its way to a lab for scientists to take a good look at the guy. Yes, my tumor is a dude. My friends named him Toby the Tumor. (Don't worry, this is not out of spite; At the time I didn't know any Tobys personally. We simply wanted to have a less scary way to talk about my tumor and decided to give him a name. To this day I have some friends ask me in random catch-ups, "Hey, is Toby still keeping it cool?" which means, "Is your latest MRI still showing that everything is stable?" Looking at Toby apparently would take some time, and I was told that the biopsy results would probably come in two weeks. Two weeks! That is a very long time to await life-changing news. And during those two weeks, there was nothing I could do except rest, recover, and wait.

Resting and especially waiting have never been my strong suit. However, I seemed to ace the recovering part! After only two nights, I was discharged from the hospital. Even now when I look back, that seems wildly short, given the complexity and invasiveness of the surgery I had just undergone. But after a few more neuro checks, another MRI, and some short walks up and down the hospital hallway, the decision was made and I got to go home.

Jeff and one of my girlfriends made the drive home a bit more bearable. New York City potholes are mean to begin with, but they are infinitely less fun after a brain surgery. Eventually we made it back home. I went straight to bed and stayed there for the better half of the next week. I will spare you the details of my first night back, but let's just say road construction in front of your apartment is the last thing you need after a brain surgery. Jeff tried to bargain with the street workers, but all we got was a pair of (pretty solid) ear plugs.

Over the next few days, I continued my speedy recovery. I leveled up from the bed to the couch. We started going on short walks around the neighborhood. My energy levels increased steadily, and after a week I decided to have friends over. They brought food, flowers, balloons, and cookies. A few days later, my friends and I even went on a hike, an unintentional seven-mile trip up and down the hills of Harriman State Park. Yes, seven miles! My friend accidentally got us lost, but it seemed like my recovery only benefitted from this.

Physically, I felt like I was almost back to normal. This was further confirmed when a physical therapist did a home visit two weeks after the surgery and declared that he didn't need to return, since I could walk around the block at appropriate New York City pedestrian speed. As part of my discharge from the hospital, someone had arranged for home visits like this one. I must have not paid attention to these instructions during my haze from pain, painkillers, and general confusion. Luckily, Jeff had listened with care and knew to expect a home-visit nurse and social worker, who called me to request appointments. Jeff also paid attention to make sure I was taking the right medications at the right time every day. These medications included steroids to decrease the swelling in my brain, pills to prevent seizures, lots of painkillers, antibiotics to prevent infection, and anxiety medications.

Why anxiety medications? Because while I was a master at recovering and getting better at the resting, there was also the waiting. And the waiting sucked. A lot. Knowing that soon a doctor would tell me whether my life would go back to normal or forever change would send my emotions spiraling every single day. I was so scared that I would suddenly burst out in tears. The anticipation of my potentially life-changing diagnosis stressed me out so much that my post-surgery headaches turned into tension headaches. It's hard to articulate just how much I struggled with the unknown.

Eventually, the long-anticipated day came. Ten days after my surgery, I was finally going to find out how much of a curveball this whole thing was going to be.

How you can support:

☞ Distract: During this worrisome waiting period, all I really wanted were distractions. Most of that time I was still fatigued from the surgery and couldn't handle light or screens, so my usual distractions (spending time with friends or watching TV shows) were out of the question. My friends got creative: One of them recorded a daily podcast for me using WhatsApp messages. Each episode was only ten minutes long, and she mostly talked about trips that we had taken and other fun memories. Another friend created personalized crossword puzzles ("4 down, short word for our favorite brunch spot") and coloring pages (based on trip destinations from our travels). Jeff bought a few jigsaw puzzles that we could solve together and got me a Rubik's cube, a challenge I had been wanting to master for a while. Identify which distractions work best for your warrior and get creative, but don't overwhelm them.

☞ Spread positivity: In addition to the awesome, creative ideas mentioned above, my friends from all over the world started sending me wonderful knickknacks. Every day their little gifts, such as comfy socks from my favorite TV show (*Friends*), made me smile. One of my friends wrote down a bunch of optimistic quotes and sent me the beautiful, handwritten notes with instructions to read only one per day. Others simply sent positive text messages. I believe in the power of a positive mindset—anything that you can do to spark positivity for your warrior (and caregiver) will likely be helpful.

☞ Expedite recovery: Because I kept complaining about my side effects from surgery, my friends tried to find small things that could provide relief: little massage balls for my sore jaw, heating pads for my neck muscles, or just calming teas to help Jeff and me relax.

☞ Provide comfort: Since my friends could predict how much I would struggle with simply resting and waiting, they wanted me to be as comfortable as possible and gave me blankets, fuzzy socks, and even cozy leggings and shirts.

☞ Keep your warrior company: It took a few days before I felt comfortable enough to receive visitors. I had to cancel plans a few times, feeling more tired than expected. But my friends didn't care. When I was ready, they came over one at a time, bringing food, cookies, and flowers, and just spent an hour or so before they suggested that I might be tired now. It was the perfect balance of distraction and rest.

Chapter 6: Five Percent

On August 26, 2021, I woke up in tears with a heartrate of approximately one million beats per second. The day of my dreaded but anticipated biopsy result discussion had finally arrived. The previous day my neurosurgeon's office had called to inform me that the surgeon, who would share the biopsy findings with me, could meet only virtually via video conference. I was still supposed to come to the hospital later in the day to have the staples removed from the scar in my head, but the surgeon would not be there. Jeff and I had spent half of the previous day debating whether this was a good sign or not. Would my surgeon share bad news over a video call? We were about to find out.

Jeff and I sat on the couch, anxiously staring at a spinning wheel on my laptop screen as we waited for the surgeon to join the session. We reviewed our questions one last time. We had one list of questions in the case that the tumor was benign (Is there a chance this will come back, even if it's benign? Could it come back as malicious? Should I be monitored for this on a regular basis? What caused this to grow in the first place?) and one list in the case it was malicious (What is my prognosis? What caused this? Will it come back, and if so, how soon? Will it kill me? What does treatment look like? Are there trials I should consider?).

The physician assistant joined the call first. She asked how I was doing. I somehow managed a faint smile . . . before I burst into tears. That's when the surgeon joined and apologized for having this conversation over video. She got straight to the point:

The biopsy results were back, and the news unfortunately was not good. My tumor was malicious. I had brain cancer.

If I remember correctly, the call took less than twenty minutes. During these twenty minutes, my life once again was turned entirely upside down. I learned that my tumor wasn't just malicious—it was extremely aggressive and had no cure. Toby's real name was Glioblastoma. Doesn't roll off the tongue quite as nicely, does it? Glioblastoma is a primary brain cancer, which means it starts in the brain and typically doesn't spread outside of the brain. The cancer develops in the brain's glial cells and forms microscopic branches that then grow into different parts of the brain. My neurosurgeon explained that it's a bit like the roots of a plant: While she removed most of the plant (the tumor), some roots (the branches) would have remained in my brain after the surgery because it's essentially impossible to remove these microscopic branches from the surrounding healthy brain tissue. The roots will try to continue to grow and, over time, allow the plant to grow back. That is why glioblastoma has a strong tendency to recur, typically doing so very quickly. While trying to process this devastating news, Jeff and I somehow managed to run through our list of questions. The surgeon hesitated when we asked about my prognosis but then decided to reveal the bleak statistics. According to my neurosurgeon, the chances that I'd still be alive in five years were 5 to 10 percent. There was a 50 to 75 percent chance that I wouldn't even make it through the next year.

It was probably at this time that I completely arrived in a state of absolute shock. I was overwhelmed by panic, sadness, and disappointment. In my head there was room for only one thought: *You have cancer. You. Cancer. Aggressive cancer.* But I tried to pay attention as the surgeon continued to explain.

She announced that the odds would look better for me if I started treatment as soon as possible. Treatment for glioblastoma typically means chemotherapy and radiation, the goal being to kill as much of the branches as possible and prevent regrowth of the tumor for as long as possible. This has been the "standard of care" treatment for newly diagnosed glioblastoma patients for decades! Yes, decades. Since you're not reading this book to become a glioblastoma expert, I'll spare you the details . . . but I do want to highlight just how scary it is that despite a lot of research, clinical trials, and other investments, there has been almost no advancement in the treatment of my very aggressive cancer. As I am writing this book, there isn't even an established standard of care for patients with a recurrence. So, if my tumor were to grow back, there would be no one proven method to try to help me. And as I found out on this video call, the likelihood of a recurrence with glioblastoma was high. In fact, glioblastoma almost always recurs. The question is usually not *if* it comes back, but rather *how soon* it comes back. While tears streamed down my face, the surgeon gently reminded us of our next steps from here:

✓   Come to the hospital to remove staples. Easy.

✓   Find a treatment team to start chemotherapy, radiation, and potential trials as soon as possible. Not quite so easy.

Then the video call ended unceremoniously with clicking a red Leave Meeting button. We spent the rest of the day taking care of these chores between several mental breakdowns. While Jeff tried to distract himself by organizing to-do lists and plans, I applied a less solution-oriented coping mechanism and kept turning into a sobbing puddle of tears. Every time I managed to calm down a tiny bit, the surgeon's words would echo in my head.

Aggressive cancer . . . rapid growth . . . difficult to treat . . . generally poor prognosis . . .

I had a lot of questions, so I spent five minutes on Google—and decided it was not the place to find the answers I wanted. The internet already suggests imminent death when you merely research a small stomachache. Googling an aggressive cancer was a terrible experience. No matter which article I clicked on, they continued to remind me that glioblastoma is a "deadly disease" that has "no cure," and the reported life expectancies were so low that it was hard to wrap my head around (most sites stated twelve to eighteen months). Still in utter shock and disbelief, I stopped my Google research and was about to put my phone away (looking at screens continued to be hard) when I saw a wealth of messages from my friends and family asking if I was comfortable sharing an update yet.

I was, but now I realized that my friends and family would probably also consult the internet once I told them the name of my disease. I decided that no good could come from scaring anyone.

So, while I wanted to tell them everything, for now I deferred to sending the following message to those who asked:

> "I have no good news unfortunately. Still processing. Sorry for not sharing anything better. It's been a day. Jeff and I are just trying to cope, but there is a plan. Radiation and chemotherapy next will take a few weeks. For now, we are going to figure out if we stick with our initial hospital or go to another one, which sounds incredibly stressful, but I just wanna get this started. The doctor's appointments today kept us busy, and I am still mostly overwhelmed. Jeff is here and we're trying to stay positive. Lots of love!"

Finally, the day came to an end. We tried to sleep, exhausted from all the emotions, rumination, appointments, and the crazy amount of uncertainty. Only one thing was certain: I needed to decide on a treatment team as soon as possible.

How you can support:

☞ Be there: As always, offer to accompany your friend to important appointments. I would have completely fallen apart without Jeff next to me for this one.

☞ Don't let the internet scare you: A prognosis is merely a likely outcome of something. The numbers and statistics that you find do not account for the specific circumstances of your warrior. That doesn't mean that you should ever downplay a prognosis, though. Just know that according to the internet, it's very unlikely that I would be sitting here writing this book right now—and yet I still am. Later in their journey, your warrior's treatment team may be better equipped to share a realistic prognosis because they will know how your warrior responds to their treatment. But I'm getting ahead of myself…

☞ Look for trustworthy and helpful resources: This is especially important if you're researching on the internet. Personally, I trust information from large cancer centers (Anderson, UCLA, Sloan Kettering) and nonprofits (American Cancer Society, National Brain Tumor Society, American Brain Tumor Association). There are a few Facebook groups, Reddit threads, and even Instagram accounts with good information. But please treat your research with care. There is a lot of false information out there and every patient is truly different.

☞ Talk about your fears—but maybe not with the warrior: Learning that your loved one has (aggressive) cancer is scary for everyone involved. It's OK to talk about that. No one should have to keep their worries to themselves. But just like with so many other topics in this book, I think there needs to be moderation here. I liked when my friends said things like, "I know you're a tough cookie, and if anyone can beat this thing it's you! But this does sound bad, and I'm scared for you." This felt like a good balance of encouragement on the one side, and acknowledgement that I had just received a devastating news on the other side. I also had friends who shared their worries about me with each other (once they had confirmed that the other person knew) rather than with me. They needed someone to talk to, but didn't want to discourage me. I love that they did this! What a great way for them to process their thoughts and feelings without putting any pressure on me.

Chapter 7: Life-Changing Choices

Choosing a treatment team and starting my cancer treatment took four weeks in total. In my entire journey of having brain cancer, I found these four weeks the most stressful, most emotional, and most frustrating and confusing yet. There are several reasons for this. For starters, I am one of the most indecisive people walking this planet. Don't get me wrong—some decisions are easy, like moving to New York, marrying Jeff (whoops, spoiler alert!), and spending most of my savings as a student traveling the world and living in different countries. But most choices are stressful to me, and I agonize over mundane decisions until the last second. One time in high school, I spent several weeks brooding over the pros and cons of getting back together with an ex-boyfriend. So, you can probably imagine just how hard it was for me to figure out which treatment team to trust with the responsibility of trying to prevent my near-term death.

On the other hand, having options is good and I was privileged to be living in a city with many great cancer centers. Over the next few weeks, I met with treatment teams of five different hospitals. Most people get only second opinions, so getting to meet with *five* different teams was truly a blessing but also a curse, due to the emotional toll and physical effort that each of the meetings involved. Securing these appointments was stressful in itself; we were on a tight timeline to get treatment started as soon as possible, but these doctors were in high demand and hard to get a hold of. Once we got an appointment confirmed, we needed to drop off a set of medical records, CDs, and paperwork a few days before the meeting so that the doctors could familiarize themselves with my case. Since we scheduled appointments in different parts of the city, we covered A LOT of ground. We probably burned off several thousand calories per day just by bouncing between hospitals to take care of administrative activities! While we were still securing some of the meetings, others were already happening.

We met with neuro-oncologists, radiation oncologists, and their respective assistants. These are the doctors who make up the core of a brain cancer treatment team in addition to the neurosurgeon. Over the course of my treatment, many additional roles got added to this team: a therapist, a physical therapist, a social worker, a dietician, a palliative care nurse, a research team, and many nurse practitioners and physician assistants. But for now, my five meetings consisted of many similar conversations with different neuro-oncologists and radiation oncologists. Every one of these meetings lasted probably an hour each. During the meetings I would be asked to go over my symptoms that led to the surgery and explain how my recovery has gone so far. Then we would proceed to do more neuro checks that had me hold more imaginary pizza boxes. Eventually the interesting part of the meeting would begin. The doctors would explain their treatment plans, potential side effects, and expected results; researchers would bring in stacks of paperwork outlining the details of their trials; and Jeff and I would ask any remaining questions. Do you collaborate with other hospitals to enroll your patients in trials? What could have caused my cancer? Do you recommend a specific diet? What will my journey look like in the long term? What are you seeing in my pathology findings that influences my prognosis? What else will determine my prognosis? What's the earliest start date for treatment? How often will I have to go to the hospital?

We frantically took notes, looking for key differences in each team's answers to consider in my Treatment Team Pros and Cons list. However, the answers to my questions were very similar with every treatment team we interviewed. They were all very skilled professionals, up to speed on the latest research, and in many cases even collaborating with other teams from different hospitals. The major difference lay in their attitudes.

A radiation oncologist at one of the hospitals essentially told me, "You probably shouldn't expect to be alive a year from now." That was a hard no right there. A neuro-oncologist at another hospital didn't even bother to look at the details of my pathology because he desperately wanted to enroll me in a trial that I had qualified for. His team pressured me to sign documents on the spot right then and there, saying that declining would mean a potential delay of life-saving treatment. But I knew that enrolling in this trial could exclude me from other trial and treatment options down the road. That situation made me feel so pressured and overwhelmed that I burst into tears, told the researcher that I was feeling scammed, and ultimately left.

Some of the teams and hospitals asked to have a piece of my tumor tissue sent to them for analysis prior to my appointment. While I partially understood this request, it was an additional stressor for me for two reasons: 1) Tumor tissue is finite. Granted, my tumor was the size of a golf ball, so there should still be a fair amount of it, but I didn't know this for sure. 2) There was a period during which I wasn't even sure where my tissue was being stored because of miscommunication between two of the hospitals I was meeting with. This clump of cells contained a wealth of potentially life-saving information for me . . . how could the hospital not know its location?! Eventually I tracked it down. I wished I could have stored it my own freezer, but for obvious reasons that was unfortunately impossible.

Between all these overwhelming, scary appointments, I still had another long list of administrative to-dos. When I wasn't on the phone with doctors, their assistants, or the receptionists, I was on the phone with my short-term disability insurance agents, trying to figure out the mechanics of keeping my job and income throughout this journey. I truly can't even imagine how patients with additional obligations handle this process, let alone parents who have to take care of young children throughout this stressful phase. Jeff and I would come home from our appointments completely exhausted from all the back-and-forth and emotional roller coasters. Sometimes we didn't even have the energy or time to eat, let alone cook. Fortunately, we have amazing people in our lives who would send us food or gift cards to order out or stop by with dinner for a quick visit.

At the end of our flood of meetings, two hospitals rose to the top. Their doctors seemed the most knowledgeable to me but also the most optimistic, energetic, and authentic. They were the only ones who suggested to do further genetic testing of my tumor tissue to look into every single genetic factor that could help us identify additional options for treatment down the road.

Finally, we made our decision on a treatment team, and a few days later I was ready to start my treatment at NYU.

How you can support:

☞ Run medical errands: This can include activities like calling medical record facilities, picking up medical records, and dropping off CDs, MRI reports, and other records.

☞ Run nonmedical errands, especially shopping for groceries: Jeff and I were truly exhausted at the end of every single day. Several friends offered to go grocery shopping for us. Others sent care packages our way. Two of my colleagues signed me up for meal deliveries and paid for them!

☞ Take care of chores around the house: If I had kids, I probably would have appreciated support with childcare. Even though I don't have kids, my household still fell apart in the early stages of my journey. Cleaning has unfortunately never been a top priority for me, and it had now officially arrived at the bottom of the list. When my best friend asked me whether I'd be comfortable with her dusting my place a bit, I was embarrassed but also extremely grateful. I didn't have a garden or pets at the time, but I'm sure those are other areas that friends and family can support with.

☞ Offer a ride: Even though I lived in New York City (in my opinion the only US city with solid public transportation), several friends offered to drive me to my appointments once I explained my logistical nightmares to them.

☞ Don't judge: I was grateful for my friends listening to me assess my treatment options. What I appreciated most was that they didn't judge me unless I asked for their opinions. No one argued when I turned down one of New York City's top cancer centers. Accept your warrior's treatment choices, even in case they decide not to get treated at all. Some cancer patients decline treatment for various reasons, and that is their right. All you can do is try to understand their reasons and support them through their choices.

Chapter 8: Love, Cyborgs, and a New Routine

My cancer treatment finally started on September 23, 2021, five weeks after the surgery. When I first learned that I'd have to go through radiation and chemotherapy, I was scared. As a kid I had watched my dad fight leukemia (he unfortunately lost his battle), so I had seen what cancer treatment can do to the human body. Several weeks of intense chemotherapy had turned him into a completely different person weighing half of his previous weight. He had slept most of the time, barely ate, dealt with skin sores, and lost all his hair. At some point it had become hard to recognize him. Would that happen to me as well?

My friends and family likely expected this and dialed up their support to the absolute maximum. I have never felt this loved in my entire life, and the memories of all the thoughtful gifts and letters I received during this initial phase of my treatment still make me smile. My mom and my best friend made the trip across the Atlantic Ocean to help take care of me. Other friends traveled across the country to do the same. They thought that Jeff and I would need help cooking and cleaning and taking my mind off things during lengthy chemotherapy infusions. Friends who couldn't come in person sent me video messages, voice messages, and letters. Others with family members who had undergone cancer treatment had practical items mailed: anti-nausea candy, colorful water bottles (hydration is key), lip balms, lotions, and cancer planners. Some friends made sure that I stayed fashionable and equipped me with lucky bracelets, colorful earrings, and pretty headwraps to cover my surgical scar. And some continued to help me rest and recover as comfortably as possible with continued deliveries of fuzzy socks, coloring books, teas, flowers, cookies, and blankets. So. Many. Blankets. Fluffy ones, silky ones, and even quilted ones. And I loved every single one of them. Every package, letter, flower, and message made my day and took a little bit of my sadness away. It made me realize how big of an army of friends, family members, and colleagues I had by my side. I was ready to fight and battle my way through tough rounds of chemotherapy and radiation . . .

But I got lucky. My treatment did not at all turn out to be the battle my friends and I were mentally preparing for. Because every person is different and every cancer can be different, cancer treatments also vary depending on several factors. Even though there is a standard of care for glioblastoma, each patient's chemotherapy dosage, radiation dosage, and radiation location depend on factors like body weight and height, and tumor location. Doctors can then add trials, off-label drugs, and supplements to the treatment plan, depending on treatment success.

When I first started treatment, it consisted of chemotherapy, radiation, and the trial I chosen to enroll in. I'll break each of these down.

Chemotherapy: I was receiving a rather small dose in pill form. So unlike some other cancer patients, I didn't have to get regular infusions at the hospital. I just took a few pills in the comfort of my home in the evening, seven days a week for six weeks. There was a strict sequence to this: Eat dinner two hours before taking the chemo pills; take anti-nausea medication thirty minutes before taking the chemo; take the chemo and go straight to bed. I barely ever got nauseous from this and never threw up. In fact, I barely lost any weight! I didn't lose any of my hair. My only side affect from the chemotherapy was a weakened immune system. My treatment team kept an eye on my blood levels because just like most chemotherapies, mine lowered my white blood cells and platelets. This made me prone to catching illnesses. To this day I am still trying to get my immune system back to normal and have caught several odd diseases in the process. And while that sucks, I'm very grateful that this was the only noticeable side effect from the chemotherapy. I know other cancer patients who deal with side effects like extreme fatigue, severe dehydration, constipation, and hot flashes from their chemotherapies, and I really feel for them and count myself lucky.

Radiation: All I really knew about radiation before talking to my radiation oncologist was that the process uses a super strong beam of energy to destroy cells. While healthy cells can repair themselves, cancerous cells are pretty bad at that and ideally die. I had a lot of questions for my radiation oncologist, but most importantly I wanted to know: How do they make sure that they don't accidentally fry areas of my brain that I need? He explained that 1) the technology was quite advanced and allowed them to radiate areas of the body very precisely, and 2) we would mold a sort of mask shaped like my face to screw into the radiation table so that it would fixate my head. Said and done— and a few days later, my creepy, Halloween-style mask was ready. I received radiation at my hospital five days a week for six weeks. Each session was only fifteen minutes long. First, the nurses would guide me to the radiation machine table and fixate my head with the odd mask. Then they'd leave the room, and the radiation machine would start whirring and moving around me. To my untrained eye, this machine looked very similar to the MRI machine, with a big, white tunnel. After a few moments of whirring, the machine would turn off, a nurse would rush in, free my head from the mask, and declare that I could now go home and rest. Sometimes radiation would give me a small headache and I would feel tired after, so I'd follow her advice. But often enough I would feel perfectly fine to grab a smoothie, hang around the park, or meet up with a friend instead of resting at home. Once again, I got lucky. While I got to sip postradiation smoothies, there are patients who deal with extreme fatigue and irritated, blistered skin.

Trial: The third part of my treatment plan consisted of my chosen trial. When I was diagnosed, there were three seemingly promising trials for newly diagnosed glioblastoma patients available in the entire New York City metro area, but I could enroll in only one. Lots of pros and cons lists, Google research, tears, and conversations with Jeff later, I chose the one that seemed most promising. The trial involved a device called Optune. In short, this device attempts to use electric fields to disrupt cell division and kill cancer cells. The patient has to attach electrodes, powered by a large battery, to their head and keep the device running for the majority of their days. Optune was by far the hardest part of the beginning of my cancer treatment. Don't get me wrong, I'm incredibly grateful to everyone involved in inventing this device, and it has likely contributed significantly to saving my life these past years. To my knowledge this machine is the only new form of FDA-approved treatment for glioblastoma since chemotherapy and radiation were approved over thirty years ago. Previous studies show positive results for patients who used the device: A significant number of patients lived a few months longer than projected when they used it as instructed. Jeff and I considered the many ways in which Optune would change my everyday life and appearance, and what using it would mean for both of us. Ultimately, there seemed to be only one answer: "Let's try it!" So, we shaved off my hair and learned how to stick the electrodes to my head. Within a day, I had become a cyborg . . . well, kind of. And I finally got a new hairstyle out of this journey!

But for the first few weeks and months, I hated everything about my new cyborg lifestyle. The device was a pretty sizeable, fairly heavy machine that I needed to carry with me wherever I went. Attached to this giant machine were four wires connected to a bunch of electrodes that were stuck to my head. All day, every day. There were several mundane things about this machine that bothered me in the beginning, adding to my continued series of emotional breakdowns. For example, imagine trying to take off a T-shirt while your head is attached to a big battery pack through several long wires. Imagine trying to go on a run or taking a shower with a bunch of wires on your head. Imagine choosing every day whether you want to do chores wearing a backpack containing the heavy device, or have only one free hand at your disposal because you're carrying Optune with the other. Cleaning the house becomes infinitely less fun. Or imagine wanting to relax with your best friend in the sun and trying to focus on catching up, but you're interrupted every now and then by annoying beeping sounds because the device overheated again. The list of surprising disruptions goes on. Optune was a continuous reminder of the fact that I had aggressive cancer and needed to learn to adapt and live with this new reality.

In the first weeks of using Optune, I was tempted to call it quits. Many days I just wanted to wrap myself in my new pile of blankets and cry. Sometimes I did just that—and was reminded of all the love and support I was surrounded with. It kept me going. My friends started to invent fun names for my new robot friend and yelled at it when it beeped.

So, with the support of all the loving people in my life, after a few weeks I finally eased into my new routine. My mornings were filled with doctor's appointments and occupational therapy, where I worked on tasks to test my cognitive abilities and improve my vision, which was still blurry. In the afternoons I went to therapy before receiving my daily dose of radiation, and then rested or spent time with friends or my mom, who was still in town. In the evenings I followed the strict schedule around eating dinner, taking my chemotherapy pills, and spending time with Jeff before going to bed.

In the beginning this new routine meant several doctor's appointments a week, sometimes even several a day. I saw on a regular basis my radiation oncologist, neuro-oncologist, occupational therapist, neuro-ophthalmologist, palliative care nurses, dietitians, social workers, and therapist, not to mention all the second opinions I continued to seek out for various questions. I talked to doctors across the country to inquire about vaccines and new trials I had read about. Some of them were just phone calls or video calls, but most of them required me to go to the hospital, where I would walk and sometimes even bike to (to the surprise of my concerned doctors).

Two months into this routine, I finally wrapped up radiation and my first round of chemotherapy. The doctor's visits became less frequent. Treatment seemed to be working so far, and we had a plan in place to keep going. After a short break from chemotherapy, I would pick it back up for one week per month and we'd keep an eye on any developments with regular MRIs. Things were finally slowing down. All of a sudden, I had time and space to reflect and process everything that had happened . . . and worry.

How you can support:

☞ Let your warrior feel your support: Just like how every patient prefers different types of support—physical (hugs), emotional (talks), material (gifts), and so forth—you as a friend also have your own way of showing your support. Do whatever feels right for you and your warrior. This bit is what matters. If you're not the type who writes letters, then offer to visit in person. But if your friend wants to be alone right now, then maybe just text them, "I'm thinking of you and am sending you a big hug".

☞ When giving material gifts, be aware that cancer treatment can take different forms: Certain lotions, for example, can be extremely useful for some patients, but other patients may not be allowed to apply them or simply don't need them. Personally, it didn't matter to me how useful a gift was. What mattered was the distraction of seeing and opening a package, and the knowledge that I had yet another person out there thinking of me. If you want to make sure that your gift will be most useful, gift cards (for food delivery services, transportation services, or online shops) are a safe bet. Or you can simply ask. I found it helpful when friends offered something specific like, "Hey I want to send you some of your favorite German candy but wanted to make sure you're allowed to eat candy right now," and I could simply respond with yes or no.

☞ Coordinate with others: You can organize bigger gifts with mutual friends. Despite the fact that I love all of my blankets, comfy clothes, and socks, I have one absolute favorite gift: a series of video messages with well-wishes. It made me smile and cry, and I have watched this video so many times. A few of my friends put this together by sourcing videos from friends, family members, and colleagues all over the world. This video helped me through so many emotional breakdowns. There are many other situations during which you can coordinate with other friends: For example, you can put together a schedule of who and when someone is supporting specific chores, offering to come over, and coming to certain doctor's appointments.

☞ Care for the caregiver: Caregivers are the real heroes in a cancer journey. Of course, as a patient I'm the one in physical discomfort; but emotionally our new normal was probably just as tough on Jeff as it was on me. He went to almost just as many appointments as I did. He made sure that I took my medications at the right time. He's the one who learned how to stick the Optune electrodes to my head. He's the one who decided to put someone else first and prioritize my needs over his. He needed and felt the support from our friends just as much as I did. You can give dedicated support to caregivers by taking them out to dinner, getting them gift cards to a spa, sending them their favorite snacks, etc.

☞ Create positive memories (before treatment starts): Once treatment starts, there are likely not a lot of opportunities to truly get away for your warrior. So, if you can, try to do something fun with them before treatment starts. Cook some of their favorite dishes, go out to their favorite restaurant, or go on a relaxing weekend trip if their condition permits. This way they can think back to the positive memories during challenging times of their treatment.

☞ Again, offer to come to appointments or cover childcare and other responsibilities during appointments: This matters mostly for patients who receive IV chemotherapy or radiation sessions at the hospital. During this phase of treatment, some cancer patients spend long days at the hospital and away from home. Helping them with chores or other commitments can be a true relief.

☞ Acknowledge the balance: Just like so many things in life, navigating a cancer journey is a balancing act. In this context I'm referring to the fine balance of support and curiosity, advice and overbearingness, and love and space. Personally, I think the best conversations occur when this balance is acknowledged. For example, one of my friends said, "I was telling a coworker about you today and she mentioned her friend froze her eggs before starting chemo. Not sure if that applies to your chemo and you're probably aware of it, but I just wanted to make sure you know about it in case you want to ask your doctor." I liked how my friend shared that she learned something that was new to her and wanted me to consider it while allowing me to decide if or when I ask an expert about it. No one should have to walk on eggshells, but during these times of heightened stress and emotion, communicating mindfully can help avoid tears.

Chapter 9: My Worry List

You might think that for a cancer patient the biggest fear must be pain, side effects, or death. Or maybe it's the fear that they could become a burden for their caregivers or be letting their families down. I'm sure if I had kids, not being able to see them grow up would have been my biggest fear. While I was tracking most of these fears somewhere on my mental worry list (except the kid thing), they never rose to the top of said list when I talked to my therapist or my support group.

Yes, in addition to all the emotional support from my friends, family, colleagues, and therapist, I had also joined a group of young adult cancer patients. I wanted to use all resources available to me to deal with this disease physically but also emotionally. While physically things had started to normalize with my newfound treatment routine, emotionally I was still spiraling. There were so many new things to worry about. I hate worrying. It's stressful and, quite frankly, usually a waste of time. And I didn't have any time to waste. Life is always short, but now that I knew just how short my life might be, I didn't want to spend any time worrying about things that are out of my control. I hoped that having a combination of a therapist, support group, and my friends would help me stop worrying and find solutions to my fears and struggles instead. So, one by one, I worked my way through the five major items on my worry list.

Worry List Item One: Legacy

I have never been worried about the process of dying. I'm sure it's not very pleasant and will cause a lot of sadness, but the fact is that we'll all die someday. That is, unless some brilliant scientist or tech person comes up with some solution to let us live eternal lives. But until then, we all will die. Many people have done it, and many more will, including me.

What scares me about death is the change in perspective that comes with it: While we live, we're all main characters in our own story. But when I think about death, I realize that I am no main character at all. I'm barely even a character, to be honest. I would love to think that all of humanity will forever remember my existence . . . but they won't. I haven't done anything to be remembered for, and I likely never will. I'm just one of eight billion people on this planet trying to do their best to live a happy and fulfilled life. All I can hope for is that the people who know me will remember me when I'm gone. All I can do is try to make small, positive impacts in my immediate environment, to be remembered for doing something good. In part, this is why I am writing this book, to be helpful to others by sharing my thoughts and humble advice. It is why I encourage everyone around me to enjoy their life and live it to the fullest. If even a few people are a tiny bit happier because of something I said or did, I'll take it. Let that be my legacy.

On the other hand, there are days where I tell myself that I should stop worrying about this legacy topic altogether. Who cares if I will be remembered or not; I'll be dead anyway. I'll never know if people create the Janice Armbrust Inspirational

Optimism Award because I won't be here to find out. While this may sound sad, it's also weirdly comforting. Sometimes I put a lot of pressure on myself, trying to leave some sort of memorable impression. But then I remember that I'll never know whether I succeeded in being a part of people's memories. More importantly, I remember that it's also largely out of my control. So, I try to stop thinking about my potential legacy and instead focus on a worry list item that is more in my control—goals.

How you can support:

☞ Tell your warrior what you'll remember: I think all of humanity could get better at telling others when they're leaving a memorable impact in any way. I don't mean this in a "By the way, when you die, I'll remember your constant optimism" kind of way. But I love when my friends tell me that something I said made a difference for them. Or when my colleagues let me know that something I did inspired them. Let your warrior (and everyone around you) know when they said or did something that changed your life for the better, even when it's something simple, like, "I'm so glad you picked up the phone when I called. I'm feeling so much better now."

Worry List Item Two: Goals

I've always been a very driven and goal-oriented person in my personal as well as professional life. And I've always worked hard to accomplish my goals, no matter how ambitious they may seem. When I was twelve years old, my best friend and I watched a TV show set in California, and ever since then my biggest goal was to live in the US. Lots of willpower, hard work, and great people helped me to fulfill this dream fifteen years later.

During those years I achieved lots of smaller wins along the way: finish high school (with stellar grades), get a college degree (with stellar grades), get a job that energizes me, get promotions, maintain and build relationships, run a 10K, spend time in South Africa and China, road trip through the US, road trip through Europe . . . I will refrain from continuing my humble brag here. The point is that formulating and accomplishing goals is part of my identity. Big goals, small goals, short-term goals, long-term goals—I had them all.

In fact, in 2021 before I got diagnosed with brain cancer, I had already formulated four goals for the next four years, until 2025:

✓   Hike the Pacific Crest Trail (PCT) from Mexico to Canada.

✓   Become a public speaker.

✓   Get another promotion as soon as possible.

✓   Move to Los Angeles with Jeff and get a dog.

I had a rough plan to tackle each of these and was excited to turn my goals into reality! However, as you know by now, a few months later I found out that the odds of me being alive in 2025 were unfortunately pretty slim. Almost overnight, my previous list had been replaced with one singular goal: Fight and stay alive for as long as possible.

It seemed irrelevant and impossible to focus on anything else. My entire life had suddenly become centered around one objective: Do everything in your power to live. This included completing chemotherapy, completing radiation, researching treatment options that my doctors might not be considering, and eating healthily. I even tried a ketogenic diet for a while because I found some research suggesting that such a diet might slow down cancer growth. I was almost thankful when my doctors advised me to stop this self-prescribed diet because I was losing weight and there wasn't enough data at the time to confirm that it truly had any effect on the outcome of my disease. Truth be told, I'm just not as happy when I can't eat my breakfast oatmeal, favorite pizza, or a good spoonful (OK, several spoonfuls) of ice cream. And what I really wanted was to *enjoy* the short time that I might have left.

So, I updated my goal once again: *Live a happy life for as long as possible—and inspire others to do the same.* This new goal meant that I wanted to be able to answer YES to the following questions: If my cancer recurred tomorrow, would I be proud of how I spent the time since my diagnosis? Would I be excited about how I spent the previous months and weeks? I have stuck with this rather broad goal since. But I still have a list of small goals for every year; like many people, I need to have objectives to know where to focus my energy and how to prioritize. Most of my ambitions now are just little things I want to accomplish to spark joy, like going on hikes and climbs, traveling to countries, or exploring new hobbies.

Would I still want to hike the PCT? Yes, of course! If it wasn't for my cancer, I'm pretty sure I would have completed that in my four-year timeframe (and maybe the other goals as well). But I do have cancer, and that means saying goodbye to some old dreams and transforming them into new ones. It's just not realistic for me to walk from Mexico and Canada in one go anymore; that would mean pausing Optune and other treatments, which would put my health at significant risk. Instead, I now plan to hike some of the trail's prettiest sections and experience as much of it as I can. It won't be the same as the very tough accomplishment of continuously hiking and beating the elements for five months. I'm sad that I didn't get to prove to myself that I can do that. But at the time of my writing this book, just a few weeks ago I hiked twelve miles on the PCT and got to camp in one of the most beautiful areas of it together with Jeff. So, I am happy. And that's my goal.

How you can support:

☞ Encourage your warrior: Not every person is as obsessive about goals as I am. But giving ourselves ambitions helps us to have something to work toward, and I think that is important when you have cancer. So, if and when appropriate (obviously not on day one postdiagnosis), ask your friend if they have any goals. And if they do, then ask: Is there something you can do to help them achieve it? Can you help keep them accountable? If they don't have goals, maybe you can help them find one for the short term, like to complete all thirty of their radiation sessions.

☞ Give room for venting: Even now, I'm still grieving some of the dreams that I won't be able to turn into reality because of my cancer. While I try to focus on the things I can do most of the days, there are days where I just need my friends to let me vent.

☞ Celebrate: And then celebrate the heck out of the achievement of any goal, no matter how small. Day one of chemo completed? Celebrate! Week one completed? Celebrate! Month one completed? You get the gist.

Worry List Item Three: Money

Glioblastoma is not only one of the fastest spreading cancers and cancers with highest chance of recurrence, but it is also apparently one of the more expensive ones to treat. While health insurances typically cover the standard of care treatment, there are novel treatment methods under development that are not yet approved for the broader group of patients. For example, when I was diagnosed, there were a few vaccine options that could potentially prevent recurrence . . . for two hundred thousand dollars. Yikes. A few of my friends instantly jumped to action and asked if they should start a fundraiser to make this vaccine a possibility for me. I decided against this because there wasn't enough data to support that the vaccine even worked—at least, not enough data for me to justify spending any of my loved ones' money on it.

The bottom line, however, is that glioblastoma, like so many other cancers, is wildly expensive to treat, and without health insurance I'd be broke or dead now. That in itself is a scary situation to be in because what if I ever lost health insurance? And what about the less fortunate people out there who may not even have health insurance to begin with? I'll spare you the rabbit hole I went down because of this question, which led me to broad, nerve-racking societal questions about privilege, ethics, and politics that could be a book of its own. In fact, there are several books and studies on these important topics. So I will move on to an aspect of my money worry list that is a bit more in my control: savings.

When you have cancer or another terminal illness, how do you spend your money? Or, in other words, how much money should you be saving when you may or may not die within the next few years? For most of my adult life, I was told to save for retirement and live a frugal lifestyle. This made sense to me—until I was diagnosed with aggressive cancer. If you have cancer, you simply have to consider this fact when making decisions, and that includes financial decisions. Does saving money for retirement still make sense? Does it make more sense to spend all my money and travel the world while I still have the ability to walk and talk? I don't know the right answers to these questions. Weirdly, no financial advisor seems to have specialized in this problem (yet). I'm sure at some point there will be health-related, data-based financial models to help people make informed decisions based on their diagnoses, but so far I haven't come across any such thing. Truth be told, I continue to struggle with this topic. All I know is that I want to be able to say that I lived a full and happy life until the very last possible day. For now, I have decided to spend the money I need to create many happy memories and then try to save the rest. One day I'll find out if that's the right decision. Until then, I'm trying my best not to worry about money.

How you can support:

☞ Help research free services for cancer patients: There are many amazing support organizations for cancer patients out there (for example, Red Door Community in the US), and some of them even offer free legal or financial advice. I personally didn't find a solution to my broad, existential question, but the resources I found were still very helpful, and I loved hearing someone tell me that I'm not the only cancer patient thinking about this. These services can also help set your warrior up with local organizations that, in some cases, provide free food to cancer patients (like God's Love We Deliver in New York City) or even sponsor cancer patients to go on adventures (like First Descents).

Worry List Item Four: Relationships

Relationships are the most important thing in my life, closely (but not too closely) followed by spending time outdoors, traveling, and feeling productive. These last three change every once in a while, which is normal as we get older, but relationships have always taken priority. Spending quality time with my best friends has been my constant pillar of happiness and gratitude. And in 2020, another constant pillar of gratitude and happiness surprisingly entered my life: Jeff. Jeff and I met at a climbing gym, right before COVID-19 shut down the entire world. And he hasn't left my side since.

So, why was I worried about relationships? There were several reasons, and they all came back to one big theme: Having cancer changes you in many ways. I was worried that these changes would impact my relationships. For starters, I was concerned that my cancer would recur and cause me to lose my ability to speak, walk, or even text. In that scenario, I wouldn't be able to communicate with my friends or my mom in Germany anymore, and I'd be limited in what I can do with my friends in the city. Would my friendships change because of that? While I've been lucky with my cancer journey to date, this scenario is a challenging reality for many cancer patients. They need their friends and families to get creative and find new ways to maintain or even improve relationships within the context of whatever hand their warrior has been dealt.

But even physically being in almost the same shape as I ever was, there was still plenty to think about. What if my friends said something insensitive to my situation? Now, you might think, 'If they are truly your friends, they wouldn't say anything that could ever hurt you!' But here's the thing: We're all just human. We can't possibly consider everybody's circumstances all the time, and we also can't know all the things that might hurt another person at any point in time. I know that my friends, family, and colleagues have the best intentions, yet over the first few months of my cancer diagnosis some would still accidentally say things that would throw me off. It could be as simple as the language they were using in a moment when I was emotional to begin with, with phrases like: "This workout was terrible, I'm so dead," (No, you're not, but I might be soon.) or "Ugh, this is so complicated. It's making my brain bleed!" (No, your brain is fine, but mine is not). You get the idea. In the early stages of my journey, phrases like these changed the interactions for me. Maybe I should have said something, but I didn't want anyone to walk on eggshells around me. I didn't want anyone to change what they would do or say because "the cancer patient" was in the room.

I also didn't want my friends to keep anything from me because of my diagnosis. With all the outpouring of love and support I was receiving, I knew that my friends understood how severe my diagnosis was and what a turn my life had taken. I knew they were worried about my situation too. And because I knew they were worried, I was worried that they wouldn't want to worry me about things. Yes, you read that right. I got scared when my friends said things like: "I didn't tell you because you already have so much going on," "I didn't want to burden you with this in addition to everything else," or, even worse, "This is such a small problem compared to what you're going through that it basically doesn't even matter." Everything that my friends go through always matters to me. I wanted them to tell me every single thing, no matter how small it may seem. I didn't want my cancer drama to stop them from sharing their own news, good or bad.

All these concerns came down to communication. I told my friends that I wanted to know whatever was on their minds, and I also spoke up when my friends said things that truly upset me. Fortunately, I can count those situations on one hand. Most of these situations occurred when friends either compared my cancer to something unrelated going on in their own lives or shared their own theories about my cancer treatment when I was emotionally in a vulnerable state. I wasn't mad at them in these moments; they simply didn't understand what my cancer journey felt like and didn't expect their words to cause me any pain.

Fortunately, a lot of people my age don't quite know what it's like to have cancer (which is one of the reasons I'm writing this book, to spread awareness of what it can be like to be a young adult with cancer). The trauma of a sudden diagnosis, the treatment, the emotional implications—it's hard to understand. That's why I like when people flat-out ask me. I like questions such as: "If you don't mind sharing, what does this machine on your head do?" "Do you still get treatment? Can I ask what that looks like?" "When is your next MRI?" "How are you feeling today?" The open curiosity of these questions lets me share my experience in a neutral light. There is neither drama nor pressure with these kinds of questions. However, there is one question that I quickly came to dislike in the early stages of my treatment: "Are you feeling better now?" I understand why people instinctively ask this question when someone is ill. People who asked me this just kindly wanted to confirm that I was getting better. However, this question was almost impossible for me to answer and put a lot of pressure on me. I was getting neither better nor worse. My cancer is not like a cold that makes you feel ill for a bit before you recover and feel healthy again. I am feeling the same (mostly healthy) every day, and at the same time I have aggressive cancer that could come back any moment. This question made me feel like I should be getting better somehow, like I wasn't doing enough to improve my situation. My response to this question usually resulted in some version of "I'm feeling pretty good today. We'll see what the next days bring. Send positive vibes." Answering how I was doing on a specific day removed a lot of the pressure and emotion for me.

Last but not least, I was also worried about my relationship with Jeff. Objectively, there was nothing to worry about. In fact, a few weeks into my diagnosis, Jeff had suggested that we get married. But I essentially told him that he was crazy. Why would anybody want to marry someone who just got told they have aggressive cancer growing in their brain? Someone weak and fatigued from surgery and treatment? Someone they would have to take care of for the rest of the cancer patient's (likely short) life? The diagnosis had made me feel worthless and like I disappointed so many people, including myself. I had thought that I was strong, smart, and healthy, and full of confidence. But now I doubted everything. I was upset with my own body. It had betrayed me, pretending to be healthy while an aggressive cancer was growing inside my brain. I was almost disgusted by the thought of it. My body was broken and had let me down. And on top of it all, I had turned into a cyborg, wires sticking out of my head and all. It was hard to imagine why anybody would be attracted to me. When I thought of my body, I imagined the battle it was fighting. It was hard to think about anything else, let alone anything intimate. My mind was occupied with thoughts about MRIs, chemotherapies, tumor pathology, and death. Not very sexy. And being plugged into a giant battery most of the day did not help. The idea of romance was the furthest thing from my mind. None of my support groups, treatment teams, or even therapist brought this topic up. But there is so much to talk about here! For example, how chemotherapy affects birth control, fertility, and hormone levels is a huge discussion point that cancer patients may want to consider when planning for their future. While that's another topic for another book, this is very important for young adult cancer patients to think and talk about with their treatment teams.

Ultimately, I shared all my worries and thoughts with Jeff. As always, talking about my feelings and concerns was a good idea. A few days later, Jeff and I decided to try to leave all cancer worries behind us for an evening and went on a proper New York City date. I traded in my comfy leggings for a cute dress for the first time since this ordeal had started. Holding hands and staring into each other's eyes, we dined at my favorite pizza spot in SoHo. It felt just like one of our first dates (except that it was late afternoon to accommodate my chemotherapy schedule). Jeff told me how beautiful he thought I was, and I believed him. Many more dates followed and eventually I was able to leave my relationship doubts behind. It just took a little bit of time, trust, and love.

How you can support:

☞ Ask and listen: Unsure if your warrior wants to talk about their cancer today? Ask. Unsure if something you said made them feel uncomfortable? Ask! And then listen, but also respect that your warrior might not have an answer. You can alleviate pressure by suggesting potential answers and options and simply asking for your warrior's preference.

☞ Share: Is your warrior saying or doing something that makes you feel awkward? Let them know. Do you feel helpless? Let them know (but don't expect solutions). Is there something "small" going on in your life that seems miniscule compared to the big elephant that is cancer? They likely want to know!

☞ Be considerate: Don't compare, don't say you know how they feel (you likely don't), don't dramatize, and don't trivialize. Not surprisingly, my overall advice when it comes to relationships is: Communicate and be mindful. Try to avoid phrases that increase pressure on your warrior.

☞ Show love: Find ways to tell your warrior that their diagnosis, side effects, or disabilities don't change your love for them.

Worry List Item Five: Cause and Prevention

Why do I have cancer? I have asked myself this question many times. Not in a "Why me?" kind of way . . . just in a "What caused my body to develop cancerous cells?" kind of way. The thing is, at this point in time nobody knows what causes glioblastoma. There is some research around genetic factors that may increase the risk of developing it, but this likely doesn't apply to me. Outside of genetics, there is currently no evidence indicating that you can do anything to cause or prevent glioblastoma. That, of course, did not stop me, or my relatives and friends, from trying to understand why I, at the age of twenty-nine, had developed such an aggressive form of cancer.

It is pointless to think about this. We can't turn back time, and I can't do anything about my diagnosis now. Nevertheless, it's very hard to stop the questions. For all of us. "Maybe it's your birth control? I read something about those hormones being bad." "It's probably because of your work. All the stress and flying across the country all the time, and all those phone calls . . . That has to be bad for your health!" "Do you think it might be the COVID vaccine? I mean, I know it's good, but it's so new and they can't know all the long-term side effects yet, can they?" It is simply none of these things (as far as we currently know). While scientists and doctors continue their research and have started to identify potential risk factors for glioblastoma, currently my doctors and I are not aware of any science that can explain why I have glioblastoma. Someday we'll hopefully know more. But until then, my friends, family, and I should just stop guessing and distract ourselves from these thoughts. Because they are painful.

For me, these conversations usually ended in tears because I felt like I had done something wrong that now resulted in me slowly dying. I felt like I was letting myself and everyone else down because I made a mistake somehow that led to me having cancer. But over time, I learned to believe in the research.

I did nothing wrong. It's hard to believe this for two reasons: 1) As the philosopher Immanuel Kant explained to us, humans want to believe in causality. It's hard to truly accept that this cancer just developed out of thin air. 2) If I did nothing to cause my cancer, then there's also not a lot in my power to prevent it from returning. I grasped at straws to find any specifics that were in my control to prevent a recurrence. Completing my treatment would hopefully help, but there must be more I could do, right? I dug through the internet, all the subreddits and Facebook groups, several scientific articles, and even some books to find things I could do. I suggested supplements to my doctors and educated myself on off-label drugs, weird protocols, and a bunch of funnily named weeds and herbs. I had binders with printouts of things I could try . . . but there was no data to back any of it up. At some point, I decided to trust my doctors and stop the obsession. It wasn't healthy.

This wasn't hard for only me to grasp. It was also hard for the people around me. "There must be something else you can do? Have you asked your doctor about turmeric?" I had. In fact, I was putting it in my oatmeal every morning. It was not delicious. And, as was the case for all the other things I had considered, there was no data to support the idea that turmeric would actually help me with cancer. Turmeric just has some general health benefits because of the curcumin it contains. Eventually I stopped ruining my favorite meal of the day. My doctors and I did agree to a few off-label drugs that I added to my regimen once we confirmed that they didn't cause me any side effects. There is a lot more that I could try and hope for the best – but I settled to try the few things my doctors recommended and that didn't impact my quality of life. With that I stopped obsessing over all the supplements and innovative treatment protocols and am patiently waiting for the research to advance.

How you can support:

☞ Avoid spiraling: Unless your warrior specifically asks you to, never ever start suggesting reasons that could have led to their cancer. I simply cannot imagine any situation in which doing so would be helpful. Just don't do it. It too easily results in feelings of blame and sadness.

☞ Be careful when suggesting "remedies": Unless you're a medical expert specializing in cancer research and treatment, you're likely not qualified to provide advice. I know that all advice is well intended and perhaps some patients appreciate it, but I'm a pretty stubborn person and don't do too well receiving unsolicited advice (I love giving it though, as you can tell by this book). Especially in the first months after my diagnosis, people telling me that I should or shouldn't eat certain things when there was no scientific foundation or support from my doctors felt confusing and stressful.

☞ Distract: If you see your warrior ruminating over the hows and whys, suggest that they could ask their doctors, who likely have the most recent science-based answers to these questions. Then it might be helpful to steer the conversation in a different direction. There is usually no use in arguing about causes or preventions with friends (except if they are scientists or doctors in the field) unless it helps your warrior process their diagnosis somehow.

Chapter 10: Back to Work

In January 2022 I returned to work. It was weird. In general, I am fortunate and extremely grateful that I work for a very accommodating company where my colleagues are just as considerate as my friends and family. But during my first weeks and even months back I struggled a little. I had expected a few challenges returning to my desk, laptop, and meetings, but some obstacles still took me by surprise. My doctors had warned me that extended periods in front of my computer could cause headaches or migraines. They cautioned that if I worked too many hours or experienced too much stress it could trigger seizures. They kept reminding me that I need to focus on sleeping, resting, and healing. Overall, they did not seem thrilled with the prospect of me retuning to work. We agreed that I would start by working a reduced schedule to mitigate some of these risks.

So, following doctors' orders, I started by working thirty hours per week. During my first weeks back I was relieved to find out that I could pick most aspects of my job back up swimmingly! But several times a day I was also frustrated with myself; things that I used to do in my sleep had become a challenge, like keeping track of my e-mails, taking notes during meetings, remembering conversations, or staying organized. I had to take frequent breaks to relax my eyes as well as my brain. The sheer volume of meetings, conversations, and information was fatiguing. I was scared and started wondering: Down the line, would I be physically able to keep my job? Would I be able to regain my organizational skills? Would I ever be able to work full-time again? Would my superiors be hesitant to give me responsibilities? Could I even be trusted to manage teams anymore? How could I work with team members across time zones if I only worked six hours per day? How would my cancer affect my career long-term? Would I ever be able to compete with all my brilliant colleagues? Would I ever be able to get a promotion again? Did any of this even matter? *Did I even care about work anymore now that I had cancer?* This last question for me was the scariest of all of them.

As you already know I used to be a workaholic; to be honest, I probably still am a little bit. I've been working ever since I was sixteen, first during high school at a little kiosk selling crepes and ice cream and selling tickets at a movie theater, then during college as a freelance trainer, statistics tutor, private tutor, and research student—all at the same time! After college I started my full-time job at a consulting firm and have worked my way up the ladder there for several years now.

It was easy to be a workaholic prior to my diagnosis. I was surrounded by workaholics, driven people, and high performers most days of the week. Work made me feel important, especially when I was flying across the country every week, zooming through airport after airport in my high heels. I was aware that what I did wasn't changing the world, but I was good at my job, and it energized me. I led large teams across the globe and delivered work for clients I respected, with leaders I loved. Sure, it was busy; fourteen hours of work in a day were no rarity. I was out of town most days during the week, crammed into planes, hotels rooms, and office buildings with colleagues and clients.

But overall, I was proud of my career and happy with the life I was living. There was no reason to pause and reconsider anything I was doing, especially since I was doing all of it in my new home country of choice. Work used to be a big part of my identity. A lot of my friendships were forged at work. Work was where I spent more than fifty percent of my day, every day (sometimes a lot more).

Until the day I was diagnosed with brain cancer.

Up until my diagnosis, I was mostly concerned with how I could become even better at my job and get promoted even faster. But now that I had aggressive cancer, I had different goals and a new perspective on life. I wanted to live a happy and fulfilled life for as long as possible. So, was it wrong to care about work at all when I might have only a few months left on this planet? How could I keep working on spreadsheets and slides when there was still so much of the world to explore? Should I just quit and travel as long as I still could? How could I justify spending my time at a desk when I potentially had so little time left to spend with my loved ones? Given that I need a salary, are any of these questions even worth asking? What expectations should I have of myself now that I had cancer?

The solution that I eventually found was simple in theory: More than ever I needed to make sure that my work directly contributed to my happiness and fulfillment (while of course aligning with company priorities – we are a business after all). To justify sitting in front of a laptop several hours each day, I needed to work on something that was meaningful to me. The time I potentially had left was too short to pour attention into things I didn't find impactful.

So, a few months after I had returned, I made a decision to take a leap of faith and pivot my career into a new direction (I'll spare you the details; they are not relevant for your mission to support your cancer warrior). While my supervisors were all very supportive, this step still took courage. Without my new perspective on the finiteness of life, I likely would have continued down my previous career path. Don't get me wrong – I was still a hard worker and still wanted to be proud of the output of my effort. I simply made more active choices regarding where I focused my time and energy in the workplace. My goal at work became to make as much of an impact as possible during the reduced amount of time I was spending at my desk.

Now, you might think, 'Great, problem solved, sounds like she figured it all out and work was a piece of cake from then on.' But it wasn't this easy. While I was quickly relearning how to prioritize, organize, and focus, there was one obstacle that I still needed to overcome: social interactions. By that I mean catching up with old and new colleagues, and clients.

Prior to my diagnosis I didn't think twice about any of these interactions. Now each of them made me hesitate: Should I mention my brain cancer? Would mentioning it change people's perception of me and my ambitions? I was scared to tell clients. What if they thought I was less capable? I was scared to tell my superiors. What if they wouldn't give me the roles I wanted? What if they treated me differently than before? What if they treated me the same as everyone else even though I had a life-threatening illness? I was scared to tell my team members and peers. What if they didn't know how to react?

I had a hard time finding the balance between telling the truth and being authentic—and keeping in mind that work is not the time nor place to share the details of what I was personally going through. I was unsure about how much health-related information was wise to share in a business environment. Bizarre situations occurred when I didn't share my news, but also when I did talk about my cancer. More than once I accidentally made my co-workers cry. It happened when people asked, "Are you back for good now?" and I would feel the need to explain that this cancer is kind of a lifelong thing because it's likely to return. Sometimes it happened simply because people were empathetic and felt sorry for me. A few times it happened with colleagues who had a relative or friend recently pass away from cancer, and when they saw my headwrap or heard about my story, that reminded them of their loss. Those situations made me feel especially sad and guilty. I didn't want to make anyone cry, and I definitely didn't want to remind anyone of their own pain. I wanted to do the opposite and spread positivity.

There was another reason why social interactions were scary now that I had brain cancer: Somewhere along the way, my cancer or the surgery decreased my ability to recognize faces. To this day, no matter the gender, ethnicity, or age, I have a hard time remembering people who I didn't know prior to my surgery. This side effect is one of the most unexpected ones for me as well as my doctors. It seems likely that the surgery has caused this condition, commonly known as "face blindness". It makes for very awkward interactions, especially at work where I meet people quite frequently and then don't recognize them when they approach me two weeks later.

Despite these challenges and concerns, I knew that I had gotten lucky once again. While it took some time, relearning, supportive conversations, and tears to rebuild my confidence at work, I was fortunate to have returned to my job. I know several cancer patients whose condition prevented them from working at all. I was determined to make the most of my situation.

How you (as a coworker) can support:

☞ Ask if you should ask: Recently a coworker said to me, "I really want to try to understand what you're going through and how your treatments are going. If you don't want to share, that's obviously fine, but I wanted to let you know that I'm interested in learning more if you're comfortable sharing." He had a lot of questions because one of his friends had just been told that they had cancer, and I was happy to share my experience.

☞ Support your warrior during critical appointments: I personally like when coworkers check in with me, especially when I have MRIs or other checkups coming up. I would tell my immediate teams about important appointments in the near-term, and they would wish me luck and let me know they're thinking of me. They also would offer to take on some of my responsibilities to cover for me during the appointments. I absolutely love that they do this. Not having to worry about work responsibilities, especially leading up to scary checkups, is such a relief.

☞ Identify what you or your company can do to help: This can include helping to navigate your company's accommodations. Truth be told, I'm pretty sure that I'm still not taking advantage of all the accommodations I might be entitled to. But I appreciate when someone offers to research potential accommodations for me or reach out to supervisors when they come across something promising. One thing I did ask many colleagues for was to connect me to coworkers who were also on reduced schedules or had chronic health issues or even cancer. These are confidential topics, and coworkers needed to agree to be connected. But the connections I made this way helped me better navigate this journey. A year after my diagnosis, a coworker connected me with two other brain cancer patients who work for my company! We started a little support group at work, which has been extremely helpful.

☞ Respect privacy: While I'm an open book, other people may be more private and want to keep health-related information private. If your warrior shares their story, feelings, or struggles with you, you should keep them to yourself, unless you were given permission to share. Even then, carefully evaluate what information is useful or necessary to share. For example, several coworkers coordinated to give me the most amazing gifts during my treatment. Whenever they did this, one of them reached out to ask if I was comfortable with them telling other coworkers about my surgery and treatment. I appreciated this consideration for my privacy.

☞ Give gifts as a team: While a few coworkers sent me food and other gifts in a personal capacity (which I *loved*), some of them got together and arranged gifts as a team (which I also *loved*). Both ways are great. However, arranging gifts as a team allowed more colleagues to pitch in, making me feel so loved and missed during my leave of absence. I received virtual postcards with small well-wishes from each of my team members, collections of podcast recommendations, and blankets. One of my colleagues went all out and organized for me to receive physical postcards with well-wishes from colleagues even outside of my immediate team, including some of our most senior leaders!

☞ Listen, acknowledge, and be compassionate: In a stressful work environment where everyone just wants to get stuff done, it can be hard to really listen and take the time to understand. Once, I was complaining to a coworker that navigating my constantly overflowing inbox was more difficult now that I had cancer. They pointed out that the volume of emails is a challenge for everyone. While that's true, it bothered me that my colleague hadn't paused to acknowledge how this challenge could be even more pronounced for me and to try to identify a potential solution with me. Similar to my other relationships, I don't want anyone to walk on eggshells around me, especially not in a hectic corporate environment. But if you know someone you work with has a disability, I hope you can pause and try to understand why a simple problem may be harder for them, and ask if there's something you could do to help (or, ideally, suggest what you could do to help).

Chapter 11: Back to Life

What would my everyday life be like living with aggressive cancer? I was scared to find out the answer to this question when I first received my diagnosis and started treatment. I knew my life would have to be different for a few months while I went through surgery, chemo, radiation, and recovery. But what would I physically be able to do after that? Would I still be able to hike and rock climb like I used to? Would I still be able to explore New York City like I used to? Would I be able to travel, drive a car, or even ride a bike? There was only one way to find out: I had to try it.

I decided to give everything a shot and started with rock climbing. In early fall of 2021, still in the beginning of my chemotherapy, I returned to the climbing gym. My doctors were not exactly thrilled for someone with a titanium plate in their head to hang on a rock wall several feet above the ground, but they also wanted me to enjoy life and be active. We compromised that I'd wear a helmet at all times (which Jeff diligently made sure of). At first, I was afraid of falling off the wall, scared that the impact would make my head implode. I started with little jumps, bouncing around the gym to assure myself that the titanium plate in my skull would hold up. Once I was on the wall, I realized just how weak I had become. Even climbing easy routes brought me to my limit fast. It was frustrating. My muscles and strength had not benefitted from all the resting and waiting. So, I started strength training. Sooner rather than later, I was back to hiking and running as well. I quickly realized that my endurance was completely gone. A few miles into my runs and hikes, I'd start feeling dizzy. During these moments my vision would start to get blurry, and my brain seemed unable to process my surroundings. Scary!

There were days when I truly hated my cancer and how it affected my abilities. At the same time, I was grateful that I still had the ability at least to try to run, hike, and climb. Many other brain cancer patients do not have this luxury. Some have strong side effects from the surgery that affect their cognitive abilities as well as motor skills. Others are unfortunately unable to use their arms or legs at all after surgery. Once again, I knew that I had gotten lucky, and I was determined to make the most of it. It took discipline and a lot of support and cheers from my friends, but ten months after my surgery I was back, even stronger than before: I started climbing difficult routes outdoors, ran a 5K, and went on a difficult thirty-mile backpacking trip with a few friends.

My friends didn't just celebrate these physical accomplishments with me. We also celebrated two other things during these few months after my diagnosis, one being my thirtieth birthday.

I'm not crazy about birthdays, but this one was special. It was my first birthday after my cancer diagnosis. My friends showered me with tons of love and went all out. I had surprise visitors and even a whole surprise party! My friends decorated the location (an event space in one of their apartment buildings) with tons of balloons and organized a photo booth station. One of them baked the most delicious cake, and others contributed all kinds of food and drinks. They had also sourced birthday video messages from my friends and colleagues across the globe. I still don't know how they managed to plan and organize all of this without me knowing. It was awesome—the best birthday ever, by far!

That is, until I had my first ever seizure. In the middle of my party. It sucked. A lot. I've only had two or three seizures during my whole cancer journey. I say two or three because my seizures don't follow a "typical" seizure pattern, so doctors remain unsure of how to quantify them. This one started with a weird feeling of déjà vu and ended with me on the bathroom floor, drooling on my friend's sweater. A few moments later, medics entered the bathroom and lifted me onto a stretcher. So, Jeff and I left my surprise party early and spent the rest of the night in the emergency room. I hated everything about that (except the fact that Jeff was there with me, holding my hand). I was so bummed that I had to leave my own party this way and didn't even get to properly thank my friends who had organized it all. I was mad at my body and my brain for failing me once again, not letting me spend the evening celebrating with all my loved ones. Later I learned that I could have likely prevented this seizure if I had slept more the previous night and eaten and drunk more during the day. We increased my seizure medication, and I was determined to not let this happen ever again. Especially at the second occasion that I got to celebrate only eight months after my diagnosis: my wedding!

Despite me calling him crazy, Jeff followed through with his idea and ended up proposing to me. I was over the moon. In April 2022, we had the most beautiful, intimate wedding with forty-six of our closest friends and family in our friends' backyard. It was a truly special, do-it-yourself kind of ceremony. While some of my girlfriends helped me put on my dress and makeup, other friends decided that our chairs needed better alignment and that the whole scenery could use more decorations. They picked flowers and collected rocks to decorate our altar, which was made up with our friends' old canoe. After one of our best friends married us (under lots of cheers and tears, by the power vested in him by the universe), Jeff and I ended up taking the canoe out for a paddle. I allowed myself to be electrode free and even had a few drinks. What a wonderful break! It felt like cancer was on nobody's mind on this day, and we all laughed, danced, and cried—happy tears for the first time in months!

When there's a wedding, there's usually also a honeymoon, right? Yes, I started traveling again. At first our trips were small, a short weekend getaway that was always a long car-ride distance from my hospital. But soon, I got back on a plane. Like so many areas of my life, flying was also impacted by my cancer. I used to be such an efficient traveler, one of those people who'd rush through security, mentally shaking my head at all the people who forgot to empty their pockets prior to the security scan. Now I was the slowest person in the entire line, holding everyone up as I unloaded all my medical equipment for Optune and explained to TSA staff how to swab the wires around my head. Planning and packing for trips became different too; my suitcases were full of medical equipment and medicine, and travel schedules had to line up with my doctor's appointments. It was annoying, but not impossible. So, we started to return to our routine of going on climbing and hiking trips.

Life finally felt almost normal again. I was still continuing my chemotherapy (once a month) and thinking about my cancer a lot (at least once a day), but overall life was good. I was relieved with the stability that had finally returned to my life, and my doctors kept delivering good news. The good news lasted until May 2022.

How you can support:

☞ Don't forget: I don't need to be showered with gifts, blankets, and loving texts all day, every day. But I still am battling cancer. I truly appreciate when my friends ask me whether Toby is "still chilling," or when coworkers want to know when my next MRI is scheduled for and how it went. It's these little questions, cheers of encouragement, and supportive messages that continue to make this journey so much easier for your warrior.

☞ Help ease back into life: At some point I believed that it was critical for me to get back into my previous hobbies. Doing so showed me that I can still live my life and gave me yet another reason to fight. Think about the hobbies your warrior used to have. Are they still able to do them? If so, can you accompany them to something to help get them started? Can you get tickets to events that they might enjoy (probably nothing intense at first)? Can you drive them to their gym?

Can you buy them little things to get them excited about starting their hobby again? Anything you can do to lower the barrier for restarting their hobby for your warrior will be helpful. Sidenote: If your warrior has trouble walking, maybe check out the place for their interest first and see if it's accessible for people with disabilities.

☞ Help develop coping strategies for disabilities: Sometimes it can be impossible to overcome disabilities. Other times it just takes a lot of patience. While I got lucky with my surgery and treatment, other cancer patients need professional help to regain their ability to speak, walk, or write. You can help your warrior with that, too. You can read a book out loud to each other, take slow walks inside the house together, or write short notes to each other.

Chapter 12: Toby Has a Sibling

On May 3, 2022, my neuro-oncologist squinted as she stared at my most recent MRI results. I was already in tears, with Jeff squeezing my hand hard. "There are some new nodules here," she said. "They are very small. But I can't see them on your last scan. Maybe it's just radiation necrosis (dead cells after radiation). I'll have to discuss it at the next tumor board . . ."

For a moment my world fell apart all over again. It felt like I was back in the summer of 2021, navigating uncertainty while running between hospitals, shipping copies of CDs around the country, getting second opinions, informing friends, relatives, and colleagues, trying to find the right words:

> "The MRI didn't go as planned, but I don't know a ton yet. It might be nothing. But it looks like Toby has a little brother. Will hopefully know more next week. Lots of movement right now with lots of appointments."

It all took me off guard. Despite the quite poor prognosis that came with having glioblastoma, I had not expected a recurrence this quickly. I had been doing so well! And my life was finally getting back on track. What would happen now? Would I have to go back to surgery? Did this mean my treatment wasn't working?

It took the doctors two weeks to come to a (rather unhelpful) conclusion: They couldn't confirm whether the new nodules were a tumor recurrence or something else. In order to know this for sure, we would have to open up my poor brain again and do a biopsy. Thankfully my doctors did not recommend that path. Even my neurosurgeon, who I had looped into the discussion since she was employed at a different hospital, did not recommend surgery. Instead, my doctors collectively decided to recommend something called "gamma knife." I had already read about this form of treatment during my time of obsessively digging through the internet. Gamma knife basically is just a super strong beam of radiation to one specific area of the brain. While I'm inclined to imagine Luke Skywalker ramming his green lightsaber into my brain, there are actually no knives or sabers involved in this treatment. Therefore, the risks of gamma knife treatment seemed small compared to the alternatives (either another surgery or simply waiting and watching). So, I went for it.

On June 9, 2022, it was gamma knife time! I took two days off work, just to give myself time in case I developed a headache or fatigue. Jeff, as always, came to the hospital with me and patiently napped in the waiting area while I hoped that Luke (just kidding—the radiation oncologists and technicians) zapped the precise right area of my brain. The procedure was short. It was very similar to my radiation sessions a few months earlier. Jeff and I were back home in no time, and I napped the rest of the day, mostly because I wanted to be kind to my brain and body . . . But the next day, since I was still off work yet felt fully recovered, we went rock climbing.

Since we all agreed to avoid surgery, to this day I don't know if I had a recurrence in May 2022 or not. It's likely that I did because whatever was developing in my brain stopped after the gamma knife treatment. This also meant that the treatment I was receiving up to that point likely wasn't as effective as we all had hoped. If, despite all the radiation and chemotherapy, my tumor was (potentially) able to grow back, then that meant something wasn't working. All my fears and worries came back at an all-time high. If the treatment wasn't working, then how much time did I have left to enjoy life? Should I quit my job, grab Jeff, and travel until I dropped dead after all?

It felt like I was back at square one. Trying to figure out new treatment options, navigating doctor's appointments, getting second opinions, wondering if I could have done something to prevent the recurrence . . . If I had stuck to the keto diet, would my brain have remained stable? If I had decided to spend two hundred thousand dollars to try that vaccine, would I be able to continue my life for longer? Should I have pushed for surgery to gather new information on my cancer? With all the uncertainties and stress, I had to remind myself once again that I cannot change the past and I should only worry about things that are in my control now.

Ultimately, my doctors and I landed on a path forward. The easiest decision was to stay a cyborg and keep Optune going. At this point in time, I had gotten very used to the machine and the little annoyances it came with barely bothered me anymore. Optune wasn't causing any harm, and maybe it was doing its job; after all, there still was a chance that the nodules were something other than tumor recurrence.

The harder decision was to discontinue my chemotherapy. After the initial forty-two days of chemo, glioblastoma treatment typically continues with six to twelve so-called maintenance cycles, in which patients receive the drug once a month for five days. I was close to completing my sixth maintenance cycle and had planned to continue with it, given pieces of research that recommend continuing for additional months. I was scared to end chemotherapy early. But my doctors convinced me that the harm that this drug could do to my body wasn't worth the risk that it may not be working for me. My white blood cells had already taken a huge hit and were struggling to come back up. My immune system was weakened. So, I stopped chemotherapy and opted for a different form of treatment: immunotherapy. Immunotherapy essentially uses a person's immune system to get rid of cancer cells. One of my doctors once described cancer as a wicked witch who wears some sort of invisibility cloak so that our immune cells can't see it. Immunotherapy boosts the magical powers of the immune cells so that they can finally see and combat the wicked witch, a.k.a. the cancer.

Instead of swallowing a few chemotherapy pills at home every once in a while, I now had to get regular infusions at the hospital. Every three weeks, I would drag myself to the hospital, hoping they'd quickly find a vein to stick an IV into. After the usual draw and analysis of labs (to monitor that my blood cells were still at acceptable levels) I'd sit in a chair for thirty minutes or so while the clear liquid dripped slowly into my arm. Jeff would try to come on his days off from work, and we'd watch *The Great British Bakeoff* while waiting for the infusion to run its course. This change in treatment was not very dramatic; I was already used to regular hospital visits for my MRIs and lab checks.

Sitting in a chair for half an hour, munching away on my snacks, and chatting with my nurses was truly not so bad. Once again, I got lucky. Once again, I barely had any side effects from my treatment. Once again, I was ready to beat the odds. Janice 2, cancer 0!

How you can support:

☞ Don't underestimate round two: While learning about the nodules was not quite as shocking as finding out that I had a brain tumor in the first place, it was still extremely nerve-racking. Loving, supportive messages, company, and small gifts in round two were just as helpful as they were in round one.

☞ Don't get discouraged: For a short moment, I thought I had lost a little bit of my usual hope and optimism. Would this recurrence mark the beginning of my decline? Fortunately, my friends and family picked me back up while also acknowledging the scariness of the situation by saying things like, "I'm so sorry you're going through this again. I know it's not what you or any of us expected. We'll take it one step at a time, all of us together. We're here, rooting for you, whatever you need. We love you and are inspired by your fight and strength every single day."

☞ Don't blame: This should be a given, but a recurrence can be emotional not only for your warrior but also for you as the supporter. Don't be tempted by questions like, Is there something your warrior (or even you) could have done to prevent this recurrence? Just like with cancer itself, there is no point in trying to blame anyone for it. Similarly, many of the other tips I shared so far apply in round two.

Chapter 13: Moving (On)

After this potential recurrence, my life finally stabilized. I had a normal New York City summer, which for me meant lots of hiking and climbing and lots of time with Jeff and my friends exploring the city. I crossed a difficult backpacking hike off my bucket list (Pemi Loop in New Hampshire), traveled to Montana to celebrate my best friend's birthday, and then finally made it back to Germany for the first time since December 2019. So many things had changed in those two and a half years: Both of my grandparents had unfortunately passed away, the world had completely transformed in the face of a global pandemic, and I was battling brain cancer.

I was scared to book my first international trip since my cancer diagnosis. In addition to my newfound luggage and airport security struggles (thanks, Optune), my other big concern was that I didn't have my usual health insurance abroad. What if something happened and I needed some sort of urgent treatment? I wouldn't have access to my usual doctors and medication. What if I somehow lost all my seizure medication or ran out of supplies for Optune? Trust me, I take packing lists to a whole new level these days. But all the stress was worth it in the end, and it was great to be finally reunited with so many of my friends and relatives who had supported me from so far away in my cancer journey. And my journey was still continuing. Jeff and I had big plans for the remainder of 2022 and 2023: We wanted to turn one of our dreams into reality and move to California!

Moving is another thing easier said than done when you have cancer. Moving across an entire continent does not make it any easier. Finding the right treatment team for me in New York City was already difficult enough. How would I transfer my care to California? How many more CDs and medical records would I have to track down and ship across the country?

Fortunately, my New York treatment team had connections—as did I. I had already been talking to a vaccine expert for glioblastoma from a Los Angeles hospital. My New York neuro-oncologist knew two oncologists at major hospitals in Los Angeles. All I had to do was drop off my CDs and medical records once I got to the West Coast. Logistically, transitioning hospitals was much easier than I had expected. Emotionally, I was still a bit uncertain. I really trusted my treatment team in New York; they had helped me to beat the odds for one and a half years at the time of our move. Would a new treatment team manage to do the same? There was only one way to find out.

Jeff and I took a leap of faith, packed all our things into a moving container, and moved to California in 2023. Another dream came true! I was finally living in the midst of palm trees and blue skies, right by the Pacific Ocean, with lots of mountains nearby to climb and hike. Soon after the move, Jeff and I checked off another goal: We finally got a dog! A sixty-five-pound retriever shepherd mix who is truly a handful, but who is also making us very happy. We named her Pemi, after our bucket-list hike. Surrounded by beautiful nature and constant sunshine, I stepped up my climbing and hiking game even more and got back into camping and backpacking despite the challenges of my cyborg situation (Do I bring the heavy batteries, or do I risk to go a few days without Optune?).

Distracted by the new environment, friendships, and adventures, I was able to almost forget about my aggressive cancer and its recent recurrence. Almost! I was still receiving my regular infusions and doing MRIs, making sure that my brain remained stable. I quickly started to trust my California treatment teams. It turned out they were just as knowledgeable, kind, diligent, and fun as my doctors on the East Coast! Over the course of my first year in California, they helped us navigate several health scares. Because, while my brain seemed stable for once, my immune system was not.

My immune system, still weakened from chemotherapy and my other treatments, had a hard time keeping even small infections at bay. My blood cell count remained rather low, even though I had received such a small dose of the toxic chemo drug. Apparently for some patients (especially females), the bone marrow, which produces white and red blood cells and platelets, never fully recovers after chemotherapy. Over the past years that my doctors have been monitoring my blood counts, my white blood cells remained especially low, leaving me vulnerable to infections. One of these infections was particularly scary and frustrating: In January 2024 I spent another few days at a hospital due to odd, cough-like symptoms and worrisome indicators in yet another set of labs. A bunch of tests revealed that I had some nodules in my lungs. *My lungs?!* I immediately panicked. Did Toby have yet another relative? Could I have lung cancer? There was no reason why I should have lung cancer. Glioblastoma is a primary brain cancer, meaning it doesn't spread anywhere outside of the brain. I also have never touched a cigarette in my entire life. But then again, there also was no reason why I should have brain cancer. Shit just happens sometimes.

A few days later, I found myself talking to yet another anesthesiologist, this time preparing me for a lung biopsy. Just as with my brain cancer, there was only one way of finding out what these nodules in my lung were: by taking a look inside. With Jeff in the waiting room and my friends and colleagues sending the usual positive vibes and virtual hugs, I fell asleep talking to yet another set of doctors. It took almost two weeks for the biopsy results to come back. I received a call from my lung specialist during a work meeting. "Your biopsy results are back!" she announced. "We still don't know what it is, but I wanted to give you a call anyway to tell you at least that it's definitely not cancer. It's likely some slow-growing bacteria . . ."

I wasn't paying attention anymore. *Not lung cancer* was all I needed to know in this moment. I went back to my meeting, ecstatic. My colleagues (we're pretty close) noticed I was beaming with joy and asked what the call was about. "I don't have lung cancer!" I exclaimed. Their faces showed shock rather than excitement. I was apparently still learning how to share my health updates and who to share it with. Cancer had become such an ordinary part of my life that I actively needed to remind myself to apply some sort of filter in certain situations. I had moved on from most of the initial shocks and worries, but that didn't mean other people had too.

Cancer had become a part of me and my daily routines. It's on my calendar, in my Instagram algorithm, and in my Reddit feeds. It's part of my conversations with close friends, family members, and sometimes even strangers. It looks back at me when I look at the mirror: Where there used to be hair, there is now a colorful headwrap. I'm reminded of it when Optune starts beeping during my meetings if it runs out of battery. I think about it when I walk Pemi, work out, and go to bed. Not in a sad way; just in an acknowledging way. I have accepted cancer as a part of me and my story. And it will be a part of me and my story until the day that I die.

How you can support:

☞ Acknowledge subtle differences: Moving, just like traveling, working, exercising, cooking, and cleaning, is different for me now. Some people may think that once a patient has completed treatment, their life returns to normal. And while my life has largely returned to normal, "normal" is just slightly different now. There is no need to make a big deal out of this, and I don't want to be packed in bubble wrap. It's the little acknowledgements like, "Hey, do you want to leave for the airport a little early so that there is no Optune stress in security?" that I find helpful and thoughtful.

☞ Be mindful of your warrior's immune system: Even when your warrior has completed treatment, their immune system could still be weak years later. Give them a heads-up for things that could unsafely affect them, like if you have a cough: "I may have a little cold. Do you want to postpone our dinner for a few days?" or if you're going to an event together: "I think there will be a lot of people. Do you want to bring a mask? I'll bring mine, too." Protect your own health, especially before spending time with your warrior so that you can keep them safe.

Chapter 14: We All Kick the Bucket

This is a chapter about death, so please take care while reading. I don't want to bum anyone out, but skipping this topic in the book, even though it's extremely subjective, would seem dishonest to me.

As you already know, I think that death is simply something all humans do at some point. Of course, when you have a disease like glioblastoma, the chances of dying sooner rather than later are rather high. My grandfather lived a life of high quality well into his nineties, so for the longest time that seemed like an achievable age to me. Now, the odds of making it to thirty-five are rather low. Low, but not zero! And, like so many other cancer patients, I am fully determined to beat these grim odds. Stable scans, an optimistic cheer squad, and scientific advancements continue to give me the necessary hope to believe that I can still make it into my nineties as well.

Despite this, I think about death almost every day. Not in a weird way (or maybe the fact that I think about it so frequently is weird in itself), but in a "Am I prepared?" kind of way. There are three sides to this question. Let's start with the boring side: Do I have the right paperwork in place? When I die, I want to make it as easy as possible for my loved ones to clean up after me in the bureaucratic sense. They will already have to deal with the pain of my death, so I want to minimize any other burden on them by having my will, beneficiaries, birth certificate, marriage license, passwords, and any other important information and documents ready to go. This includes letting someone know where to find these documents. While these conversations are not easy, they are absolutely necessary. And truth be told, I find these topics way easier to deal with than the next side of my preparedness for death question, the emotional side: Am I living the life that I want?

When I die, I want to have no regrets. Wouldn't it be nice to know how to do that? Wouldn't it be nice to know what it means to live your life to the fullest? Will I regret that I didn't just quit my job and travel the world for the rest of my days (likely broke and without proper cancer treatment)? Or will I be happy that I lived a longer life of very joyful mediums, with my wonderful husband and my cute dog, going on adventures whenever the time and budget are right? We don't know what we will regret, and we don't know what our lives could be like if we had chosen a different path at one of the many crossroads in our stories. Instead, when I think about if I'm living the life I want, I focus on the small picture. I pause often and reflect on the choices I recently made. Do they all allow me to make the most of my life (in a sensible way)? If so, I have nothing to regret and I am grateful for the life that I get to live.

Then there is the ugly side of being prepared for death: What will happen to me? There's a pretty good chance that glioblastoma will one day kill me. Of course, other things could get in the way of that, but realistically I will die from glioblastoma. One day I asked my palliative care nurse what this death would look like. She was surprised that I wanted to know this and said, "Why are you asking me this today? You're doing so well. You shouldn't be worried about this right now." I told her that I was simply curious. I figured it couldn't hurt to learn this while I'm fully conscious and feeling healthy. That way when I do decline, I would know what to prepare myself and my loved ones for. So, she let me know that dying of glioblastoma is unfortunately a rather gruesome and potentially lengthy process. I learned that I'd slowly lose the ability to speak, move, and eat. I'd start to drift in and out of consciousness and potentially experience seizures. Ultimately, I'd stop drinking water and stop breathing. Yikes. While that sounds more than unpleasant for Future Me, it sounds even worse for my loved ones, who will have to watch me go through that process. I wish I could spare them (and myself) of this kind of death. But the images my nurse painted for me will likely turn into reality one day, and I think knowing about the process personally helps me to be prepared and to prepare my loved ones for when the time comes. Hospice teams typically work with patients and families during this last stage of a cancer journey. I'm hoping that they'll be able to keep the pain for everyone involved to a minimum.

And then I'll be gone. Chances are high that I'll turn into a tree because I'm planning to have my ashes mixed with local soil to support reforestation. I'm hoping that everyone who I have ever known, impacted, or inspired in any possible way will get together and share funny and embarrassing stories about me (there are a lot of those). I'm hoping that my closest friends will celebrate my birthdays together and share their favorite memories. Recently Jeff and I came across a few climbers who carried a bench up a mountain and to a climbing crag in loving memory of their friend, a strong climber who had recently passed away. What a wonderful memorial.

Hopefully there is still a long time between today and the day that I become a tree. While I do want to be prepared for that day, I absolutely plan to live in the present and embrace every moment of my life. I will fight hard to prevent that day from arriving anytime soon. I still have a lot of things that I want to accomplish and a lot of days that I want to enjoy life. One day I'll die—but not today.

How you can support:

☞ Live your life: Being hyperaware of my (and everyone else's) mortality, I want all of my friends, relatives, coworkers, acquaintances, and basically just everyone to live a fulfilling life, whatever that means to them. There is no right answer to this. A fulfilled life can look a million different ways. Just think about the choices you're making and do more of what makes you happy.

☞ Dare to talk about death: Years before she passed, my grandmother had wanted to talk to me about her passing. At that time I wasn't aware that she had received a diagnosis of any kind. I kept telling her, "No, Grandma, you're gonna live well into your hundreds. We don't need to talk about this!" I thought this would be encouraging for her. Turns out that was a stupid idea. She passed a few years later and it took our family a long time to piece together her will and wishes while we were dealing with the sadness of her passing. Lesson learned: If your loved one wants to talk about death, please try to respect this wish.

☞ **If you're close, offer to help with the boring stuff:** This one is tricky but so important. If your warrior has a severe illness that may cause them to decline rapidly, it's critical that they make important decisions while they are still in a good mental state. I wish doctors would bring this topic up, but none of mine have so far, except for health-related decisions (think health proxy and advance directive). I wish they would say things like, "Hey, while you're doing so well, you should make sure to get a will set up and appoint your beneficiaries." In the absence of my doctors saying this, I have appreciated careful nudges from my relatives whenever the timing was appropriate: "I know you won't need it for a very long time, but I just wanted to make sure you were putting a will in place, just in case. I'm sorry if this makes you sad and I really don't want it to, but it's just so important to think about these things . . . and I have one too! I'm happy to talk to you about it and help you figure it out if you want help. Love you tons!"

☞ **If you're close, support with hospice decisions:** Once it seems clear that treatment is failing, hospice teams should get involved to relieve pain and provide emotional support. Starting hospice from a patient's standpoint can obviously be extremely scary because it likely means that the person doesn't have much time left to live. There are patients who refuse hospice care as well, sometimes because they prefer to die in the comfort of their home. In a situation like that, you should try to be understanding, supportive, and respectful. There is no point in arguing, and no one should receive hospice care against their will; but you can listen, validate emotions, and provide reassuring facts. At the same time, though, you can ask why they're not comfortable with hospice and potentially offer alternatives. With permission you can offer to arrange for a meeting with hospice to get a consultation.

☞ Get a will: To be honest, we all should have a will in place, and we all should think through our end-of-life plan. Every single one of us. We should document what we want to happen with us, our bodies, our belongings, and our families if we die. Anything can happen at any moment in time. There are checklists for this on the internet and even TED talks!

☞ Get professional help: This applies to every topic in this book, but it applies to this chapter in particular. People go to therapy for all sorts of problems. As someone with a degree in psychology, I generally think that most humans (myself included) can only benefit from therapy. But losing someone close to you is absolutely a reason to speak to a therapist and get professional support to work through your loss.

☞ Be there for each other: Obviously. No explanation needed here. Be there for significant others, caregivers, children, mothers, fathers, best friends, brothers, sisters, and everyone who needs support. Give hugs, share stories, and take on chores. Divide and conquer, and pick each other up.

Chapter 15: Today

Today is a random Monday in July 2024, and I am feeling completely normal. What does normal mean for someone who has aggressive brain cancer? I mean, what does normal feel like for anyone these days, really? For me, normal means that I feel content and slightly tired. I just spent a long weekend hiking and climbing in the Santa Monica mountains with Jeff, our friends, and Pemi. We also spent a whole day at the beach, with Optune beeping frantically away by my side, not happy about the sunshine and heat. Today I worked a little over six hours (damn it!) and then went out to a romantic dinner with Jeff. He is now asleep on the couch, and I am writing this last chapter with Pemi snoozing by my feet.

Normal also means keeping track of my doctor's appointments. Next week I'm scheduled for my monthly immunotherapy infusion, and in August I'll be getting my next MRI. In between these appointments, I'll let my doctors know about any unexpected symptoms I experience. I am getting MRIs every two months at this time because my brain has been fairly stable (let's keep it that way, please). This doesn't make the MRI appointments any less scary; I still have "scanxiety" leading up to each appointment. A few days before my MRI I start becoming hyperaware of any changes to my hearing or vision, or any headaches I'm experiencing. Every time I think about the upcoming appointment, my heart starts beating faster. That will probably never go away. When I have an MRI appointment come up, I tell my closest friends, family and colleagues (and anyone else who wants to know) the date so that they can send positive vibes. Then the day of the appointment comes. While I am a true expert in getting the MRIs now (I know exactly which music to pick to avoid jazz), I am still nervous. Jeff still comes to every single MRI appointment with me. Usually my neuro-oncologist enters the room and spares us the suspense. "Your scan looks great" has been her way of saying hello these last few months (again, let's keep it that way, please). After the appointment Jeff and I go to our favorite café and celebrate with coffee, lunch, and tasty pastries.

Normal also means my continued struggle of trying to spend the majority of my time on things that are meaningful to me, make me happy, and inspire others. I have learned that this is called "survivor's guilt." I have two problems with this phrase: 1) I don't consider myself a survivor, since there is currently no cure for glioblastoma. This is me being nitpicky, but truthfully it seems inaccurate to call myself a survivor as long as there's a high likelihood that my cancer could recur any moment. That's why I prefer the term "warrior." 2) I don't like feeling guilty. Feeling guilty does not at all compute with my goal to be happy. But unfortunately, it's true. When you have cancer, feelings of guilt become somewhat normal. For me, they often go hand in hand with gratitude. I feel guilty for causing pain for my loved ones, but I am extremely grateful that they are happy to help and support me. I feel guilty knowing that other glioblastoma patients have strong side effects or are long gone, but I am grateful that I still get to be here and live my normal life (which is called "privilege guilt"). I also feel survivor's guilt toward myself. It's the feeling that I get when I don't live up to my new expectations.

It's the stress that I feel when I once again put in too many hours at work, despite knowing that life is short and I want to live it to the fullest.

A few months ago, I read that giving back to a community is one way to combat survivor's guilt. So, ever since I've moved to California, I've started giving back and advocating for brain cancer patients. I joined many awareness walks and events organized by the National Brain Tumor Society. I wrote a short article to share the story of how my diagnosis has impacted my goals. I became an ambassador for Novocure, the company behind my lifesaving Optune device. I did an interview with my neuro-oncologist and shared my experience with Optune to help fellow brain cancer warriors decide if they want to use it. I started volunteering for an organization called Imerman Angels, which matches cancer patients with similar stories to support their cancer journeys through mentorship. Recently I even virtually met with California congressmen to share my story and advocate for a bill related to brain cancer.

When I'm not volunteering, I am doubling down on my rock climbing, hiking, and traveling goals. For the remainder of 2024, Alaska, Austria, and Australia are on the travel destination list (no, I do not pick my destinations according to the alphabet but rather according to my friends' wedding schedules). Traveling is still more stressful than it used to be, and I am still learning to give myself grace when exercising. But this is my new normal.

Sometimes I wonder what my life would be like without cancer. I can't help but imagine that I'd still be a workaholic in New York City. Maybe I would have hiked from Mexico to

Canada this year? Then again, maybe my relationships and friendships would be weaker without the hardships we experienced together. I will never know. The only thing I do know is that despite my brain cancer, I got lucky—and I absolutely love my life.

How you can support:

☞ Help your warrior understand and work through feelings of guilt: Yes, this is another therapy one. But it's so important because many people don't understand what these feelings are. Concepts like survivor's guilt and privilege guilt are not often talked about with treatment teams. It took me almost three years to realize that most of the items on my worry list were, in fact, guilt related. I wish one of my friends had known and could have given me the words "survivor's guilt" as a term to look into and discuss with my therapist.

☞ Share your own feelings of guilt with someone: Just like cancer patients can feel guilty, caregivers, friends, and family members also can feel guilt. It could be guilty in a "Why them and not me?" kind of way, or guilt for certain thoughts around caregiver fatigue or compassion fatigue. There are lots of anonymous posts on Reddit from caregivers who feel extremely fatigued by their responsibilities and emotional burden. That is totally understandable and valid and should absolutely be discussed (ideally with a therapist). It can be hard to voice these thoughts and feelings, but don't keep it in.

☞ Advocate: Join your warrior in their efforts to advocate and volunteer, or do it on their behalf if they can't. You can donate to the many wonderful cancer organizations or other causes relevant to your warrior. Celebrate cancer awareness months or days with them. My friends join brain cancer awareness walks and runs with me (and if I can't make it, they even go without me). One of my friends currently is going all out and running the New York City Marathon on my behalf, raising funds for the National Brain Tumor Society.

☞ Continue to show up: Even if I magically live another thirty years with my cancer, I'll still want my friends to ask when my next scan or other important appointments are. We all should try to be attentive and kind. Remember important moments for your loved ones and tell them you're thinking of them. For someone with cancer, many of these moments might just be doctor related. I hope my friends will celebrate clean scans with me for many years, and I hope that they will shower me with love and support again if and when Toby returns—hopefully a very, very long time from now.

Additional Thoughts

There are a few topics that I have not touched on in this book, but they absolutely matter. Among others, these topics include religion, privilege, and health care systems.

Regarding religion: When talking about hardships, life, or death, religion will matter to many people in different ways. There are so many different perspectives, preferences, and emotions related to this topic that I don't have any specific advice, except to be accepting and kind. I personally appreciated all the prayers that my friends sent my way, no matter for which religion.

The topic of privilege truly could be a book of its own and could have come up in every single chapter of this one. Every time that I count myself lucky, I am well aware that others are not as lucky. One of the reasons for this is unfortunately privilege. The outcome of a cancer diagnosis is partially dependent on privilege: Having access to great doctors, effective medicine, and big hospital systems that can afford to invest in research and trials is a big game changer when it comes to beating this nasty disease. Simple factors like your location (rural and far away from leading cancer centers versus in a large metro area with a variety of treatment options) can impact someone's access to care and, therefore, the outcome of their illness. But the extent of this problem goes way further: There are patients who are being evicted because of the financial burden of cancer treatment. And there are patients who decide to stop treatment due to the financial burden. This needs to change, and I have started advocating for bills that may help solve some of these issues.

Lastly, there are a lot of details regarding cancer treatment, research, health insurances, and hospital systems that I did not include in this book. All of these topics can be extremely hard to navigate and are also dependent on each warrior's situation. As I am writing this book, there are bills being proposed to US Senate and Congress to help with a few of these aspects in the bigger picture. Hopefully cancer journeys one day will be less stressful and a lot easier to navigate than the start of mine.

Closing Remarks

Thank you for reading my book. I truly hope that you found it insightful and that it will help you support your warrior through their journey. Remember that each cancer journey is unique—as is mine. Take my advice with a grain of salt. We're all just human beings trying to do our best to help each other and help ourselves. Communicate mindfully, be kind, respectful, and supportive, and you will likely be an asset in your warrior's fight. Good luck, and positive vibes to you and them.

Acknowledgments

To Jeff—thank you for all the laughter, tears, and everything in between. I am forever, adoringly, yours.

To Mom—thank you for raising me to be the person I am today and loving me as I am. To Juergen—thank you for always taking care of us. And to Jeff's mom, for all the love and care packages.

To Dad—I wish you were here.

To Liz, Brittany, and Alison—thank you for being at the top of the cheer squad. I appreciate it all and hope others do too when they read about your great support ideas in this book.

To Sina—thank you for love, friendship, and support since 1998.

To John and Laura G., Dustin, Eva G., Ilya, and Frida—thank you for literally *always* being there for us, whatever we need. And for always cheering us up.

To Nikki, Helena, Katrin D., Oli S., and Max B.—thank you for being amazing listeners and enthusiastic supporters.

To Sheela A.—thank you for keeping me motivated to write this book. I couldn't have done it without my writing shirt.

To Nicole and the rest of the Boops—thank you for introducing me to the man of my dreams, and for everything else. And to the "bro chat", Jen A., and Joana (Joma) for always being there for Jeff (and me).

To Lauren K., Grace, Mima, Mark, Martin, and so many other N3Q-ers—thank you for sourcing so much love and support (and food) from our wonderful team. And to Tara, Krystle, Kylie, and the team for a box full of sunshine. And to DJB, Kavya, and the whole crew, for keeping me entertained.

To Elizabeth L.—I still don't know how you managed to get some of these well-wishes, but I appreciate them to this day and am looking at the stack of cards right now.

To Krista W., Kat N., Dave S., Kristin S., Alex M., Chelsea M., Kathrin S., Vanessa S., and Molly R..—thank you for your love and wonderful surprises.

To Kaitlyn Z.—thank you for always asking thoughtful questions and motivating me to keep writing. And to Jovana, Eugen, John K., and Michaela, for always sending positive vibes from afar.

To Nathaniel and Jeannie—thank you for teaching me how to tell a story. Hopefully this one wasn't too long ;)

To Dr. Sharma, Dr. Cordova, Dr. Barbaro, Dr. Sulman, Dr. Cloughesy, Dr. Germano, Dr. Galgano (Mike), and Dr. Kesari—thank you for believing in me and keeping me alive. And to all the wonderful nurses and other treatment team members involved.

And, last but not least, to Olivia—thank you for helping me through the writing process. This book would not exist without you. And to Lucy for introducing us.

About the Author

Janice Armbrust lives in Los Angeles with her husband and cuddly shepherd-retriever mix. In August of 2021, her life was turned upside down when she received a brain cancer diagnosis. Fueled by the unwavering support of her friends, family, and colleagues, Janice has been beating the odds ever since.

Janice is available for speaking engagements. You can reach her at JaniceArmbrustAuthor@gmail.com